Lecture Notes of the Institute
for Computer Sciences, Social Informatics
and Telecommunications Engineering   53

Ibrahim Baggili (Ed.)

Digital Forensics and Cyber Crime

Second International ICST Conference
ICDF2C 2010
Abu Dhabi, United Arab Emirates, October 4-6, 2010
Revised Selected Papers

 Springer

Volume Editor

Ibrahim Baggili
Advanced Cyber Forensics Research Laboratory
College of Information Technology
Zayed University
Abu Dhabi, United Arab Emirates
E-mail: ibrahim.baggili@zu.ac.ae

ISSN 1867-8211   e-ISSN 1867-822X
ISBN 978-3-642-19512-9   ISBN 978-3-642-19513-6 (eBook)
DOI 10.1007/978-3-642-19513-6

Springer Heidelberg Dordrecht London New York

Library of Congress Control Number: 2011922835

CR Subject Classification (1998): K.5, K.6.5, K.4.1, J.1, I.4-5, D.2.0, C.2.0

Typesetting: Camera-ready by author, data conversion by Scientific Publishing Services, Chennai, India

Printed on acid-free paper

Springer is part of Springer Science+Business Media (www.springer.com)

Preface

The Second International ICST Conference on Digital Forensics and Cyber Crime (ICDF2C 2010) was hosted in Abu Dhabi, United Arab Emirates, during October 4–6, 2010. The conference was attended by over 100 international participants including academics, senior government officials from the UAE, and corporate attendees. ICDF2C 2010 attracted significant media attention and was featured in prestigious media outlets such as *The National, Gulf News, Al Bayan, Khaleej Times* and Abu Dhabi TV.

The conference program showcased credible, peer-reviewed academic research paper presentations, industry speakers, and two tutorials.

Keynote presenters of this year's conference were exceptional experts of the field. Paul Kurtz, a world renowned cyber security expert, former Assistant to the President of the United States and Senior Director for Critical Infrastructure Protection in the White House Homeland Security Council, presented on the first day. Marcus Rogers, research scholar, professor, and a fellow of CERIAS, delivered his keynote address on the second day. The third day tutorials addressed special topics in digital forensics. The session presented by respected scholar Nasir Memon from NYU-Poly focused on the latest advancements in digital image forensics. The second tutorial led by Bhadran V.K., Director of the Resource Centre for Cyber Forensics in India, concentrated on issues of network forensics.

Special guests of the UAE's Ministry of Interior and the Ministry of Justice also honored the event with their presence: His Excellency Major General Khalil Dawood Badran; Lt. Colonel Al Shamsi; His Honor Dr. Mohamad Obaid Al Kaebi, Judge of Fujeirah Court; His Honor Dr. Omar Obaid Algoul, Judge of Ajman Court, and Dr. Suleiman Al Jassim, Vice President of Zayed University.

ICDF2C 2010 received generous support from the UAE Ministry of Interior and various corporate sponsors. The recognition of such an important event by the Ministry of Interior showed great dedication to studying and resolving the issue of cyber crime in the United Arab Emirates. ICDF2C 2010 as a flagship event in the diverse field of digital forensics greatly contributed to encourage the dialogue between science, government, practitioners and business.

Organization

General Chair

Ibrahim Baggili — College of Information Technology, Zayed University, UAE

Steering Committee

Imrich Chlamtac (Chair) — President of Create-Net
Sanjay Goel — University at Albany, USA

Publicity Chair Middle East

Manar AbuTalib — Zayed University, UAE

Sponsorship Chair

Zayed University's Development Office

Local Arrangements Chair

Zayed University's Development Office

Publicity Chair USA

Sanjay Goel — University at Albany, USA

Publications Chair

Nasir Memon — NYU-Poly (Polytechnic Institute of New York University), USA

Conference Coordinator

Edit Marosi — ICST

Technical Program Committee

Mohamed Abou El Saoud — Carleton University, Alcatel-Lucent, Canada
Michael Adlem
Steve Anson — Forward Discovery, USA-UAE

Table of Contents

Dealing with the Problem of Cybercrime

Ali Alkaabi, George Mohay, Adrian McCullagh, and Nicholas Chantler

Information Security Institute, Queensland University of Technology, GPO Box 2434,
126 Margaret Street, Brisbane, QLD 4001, Australia
a.alkaabi@isi.qut.edu.au,
{g.mohay,a.mccullagh,a.chantler}@qut.edu.au

Abstract. Lack of a universally accepted and comprehensive taxonomy of cybercrime seriously impedes international efforts to accurately identify, report and monitor cybercrime trends. There is, not surprisingly, a corresponding disconnect internationally on the cybercrime legislation front, a much more serious problem and one which the International Telecommunication Union (ITU) says requires 'the urgent attention of all nations'. Yet, and despite the existence of the Council of Europe Convention on Cybercrime, a proposal for a global cybercrime treaty was rejected by the United Nations (UN) as recently as April 2010. This paper presents a refined and comprehensive taxonomy of cybercrime and demonstrates its utility for widespread use. It analyses how the USA, the UK, Australia and the UAE align with the CoE Convention and finds that more needs to be done to achieve conformance. We conclude with an analysis of the approaches used in Australia, in Queensland, and in the UAE, in Abu Dhabi, to fight cybercrime and identify a number of shared problems.

Keywords: Cybercrime, Computer Crime, CoE Convention on Cybercrime.

1 Introduction

Grabosky, Smith and Dempsey [1] note that the "fundamental principle of criminology is that crime follows opportunity, and opportunities for theft abound in the Digital Age". Grabosky [2] indicates that the growth of computer technology and the Internet have increased the opportunities for criminals to commit cybercrime. While the general problem posed by cybercrime has been known and identified for sometime now, there are markedly different interpretations of the nature of cybercrime [3]. Cybercrime has historically referred to crimes happening specifically over networks, especially the Internet, but that term has gradually become a general synonym for computer crime, and we use these two terms as synonyms except where we make explicit otherwise. Another synonym still, one that is increasingly being used, is the term 'hi-tech crime' which makes explicit that such crimes include crimes involving any device incorporating an embedded digital device. Unfortunately, in developing more detailed and precise definitions and taxonomies, different countries and national and international organizations have given rise to diverse and often inconsistent definitions and taxonomies. In fact, the United Nations (UN) [4] noted that the problems surrounding international cooperation in the area of computer crime include the lack of global agreement on what types of conduct should be designated as computer crime and the lack of

I. Baggili (Ed.): ICDF2C 2010, LNICST 53, pp. 1–18, 2011.

global agreement on the legal definition of criminal conduct. Without common agreement or understanding on cybercrime definitions and taxonomy, it is difficult to report on its nature and extent consistently from one country to another, and to monitor trends in an informed manner. Furnell (2001) [3] notes that having a consistent classification of cybercrime would be beneficial to individuals and organizations concerned with countering the problems of cybercrime, and to those concerned with reporting these kinds of offences. The G8 [5] has recommended each country to map its high-tech crime taxonomy to "make it addressable with other countries".

Section 2 of the paper discusses the variety of terms, definitions and taxonomies used to describe cybercrime, including ones used by international organizations such as the UN and Council of Europe (CoE). Section 3 presents our refined and extended cybercrime taxonomy and demonstrates its utility and broad applicability. Section 4 explores the influence of the CoE Convention on Cybercrime (CoE Convention) internationally by analysing how the USA, the UK, Australia and the UAE[1] conform to the CoE Convention. These four countries represent a spectrum of development and culture and have been chosen partly for those reasons. Our results show not surprisingly that more needs to be done in order to address harmonization of cybercrime legislation amongst these four countries and, by extension, globally. As part of our analysis of how the fight against cybercrime is proceeding globally, Section 5 concludes the paper with a comparison of the approaches used by the Queensland Police Service in Australia and by the Abu Dhabi Police service in the UAE to fight cybercrime. The analysis shows that resourcing is a problem, and so too is reporting of cybercrime.

2 Terminology and Taxonomies

There are, at present, a large number of terms, definitions and taxonomies proposed or used to describe crime involving computers. The terms include *computer related crime, computer crime, Internet crime, e-crime, digital crime, technology crime, high-tech crime, online crime, electronic crime, computer misuse*, and *cybercrime*. The latter has been widely used recently [3, 6-13].

Symantec Corporation [14] defines cybercrime broadly as "any crime that is committed using a computer or network, or hardware device". This is a very broad definition that not only includes crimes that use or target computer systems and networks, but it also includes crimes that happen within a standalone hardware device or computer. Kshetri [15] analyses cybercrime and its motivation in terms of cost-benefit to the cyber-criminal and defines cybercrime as a crime that utilizes a computer network during the committing of crimes such as online fraud, online money laundering, identity theft, and criminal uses of Internet communication. Wall [16] describes cyberspace and the new types of crime as "new wine, no bottles", however, in contrast, Grabosky [17] suggests that it is a matter of "old wine in new bottles", since the cybercrime is "basically the same as the terrestrial crime with which we are familiar". However, generally and as indicated previously, the term 'cybercrime' involves not only new crimes against computer data and systems, but it also involves traditional crimes such as fraud.

---

[1] This research is funded by the Abu Dhabi Police, UAE.

The CoE Convention classifies cybercrime into four main categories [18]: offences against confidentiality, integrity and availability of computer systems and data; computer related offences (forgery, fraud); content related offences; and offences related to infringements of copyright and related rights. We note that the CoE cybercrime categorization does not include some types of crimes that have been committed or facilitated using the computer such as money laundering, identity theft and storing illegal content.

The UN manual on the prevention and control of computer-related crime [4], published in 1999, lists five common types of computer crime: fraud by computer manipulation; computer forgery; damage to or modification of computer data or programs; unauthorised access to computer systems and services; and unauthorised reproduction of legally protected computer programs. Though the UN manual includes crimes against computer data and systems, it also covers some crimes that utilize computer systems such as fraud and forgery. However, the manual does not refer to other types of offences that are committed or facilitated by a computer or computer system such as identity theft, money laundering and storing illegal content.

The U.S. Department of Justice defines [19] *computer crimes* as "crimes that use or target computer networks, which we interchangeably refer to as 'computer crime,' 'cybercrime,' and 'network crime'", and refers to viruses, worms and Denial of Service attacks. The UK Association of Chief Police Officers (ACPO) [20] has defined e-crime as the "use of networked computers, telephony or Internet technology to commit or facilitate the commission of crime", which is consistent with the original, network-specific, origins of the term cybercrime.

The above terms and others are often used interchangeably to describe the same crimes [6, 21], nonetheless there is an ongoing debate on the specific kinds of crime encompassed by cybercrime. Brenner [22] classifies cybercrime into three categories: the use of a computer as a target of criminal activity (e.g., hacking, dissemination of viruses and worms), the use of a computer as a tool or instrument used to commit a criminal activity (e.g., online fraud, harassment), and the use of a computer as incidental to the crime (e.g., data storage for a drug dealer to monitor sales and profits). Some others concur with this view (Symantec Corporation [14], Gordon and Ford [8], Sukhai [23], Kelly [7], and the Australian Centre for Police Research [21]). Still others however classify cybercrime into only two categories (see Koenig [24], Furnell [3], Wilson [25], Lewis [26], and the Australian High Tech Crime Centre [27]). Similarly, the Foreign Affairs and International Trade of Canada [12] classifies cybercrime into two categories: crime that is committed using computers and networks (e.g., hacking and computer viruses) and traditional crime that is facilitated through the use of computers (e.g., child pornography and online fraud). The crimes which cover the indirect use of computers by criminals (e.g., communication, document and data storage) are termed computer-supported crime and not cybercrime [12]. Likewise, the categorization by Urbas and Choo [28] identifies two main types of cybercrime: crimes where the computer is a target of an offence (e.g., hacking, terrorism) and crimes where the computer is a tool in the commission of the offence (e.g., online fraud, identity theft). Urbas and Choo elaborate the second type, the computer as a tool, based upon the level of reliance on technology: computer-enabled crimes, and computer-enhanced and computer-supported crimes.

Other classifications still have included consideration of factors other than the role a computer system plays in the committing of computer-related crimes. These factors include: threats (Thomas [29]), attackers (Kanellis et al [30]), attacks (Kanellis et al [30], Chakrabarti and Manimaran [31]), motives (Kanellis et al [30], Thomas [29] and Krone [32]), and victims (Sukhai [23]).

In summary, the overridingly predominant view is clearly that for a crime to be considered as cybercrime, the computer or network or digital device must have a central role in the crime i.e., as target or tool. This precludes crimes in which the computer has only an *incidental* role such as being the repository of either direct or circumstantial evidence of the crime and Section 3 of this paper is therefore based upon the premise that cybercrimes involve a computer system or network or digital device in one or both of the following two roles:

- *Role I*: the computer is a target of a criminal activity
- *Role II*: the computer is a tool to commit a criminal activity.

3   A New Model for Classifying Cybercrime

This Section presents the development of a more comprehensive model to character- ize cybercrime based not only upon the role of the computer, but also on the detailed nature of the crime, and contextual information surrounding the crime. Sub-section 3.1 refines the Role I/II classification of cybercrime, which we will henceforth refer to as the Type I/II classification, into a number of sub-classes and uses that refined classification scheme to categorize a comprehensive list of common cybercrimes. Sub-section 3.1 also discusses how cyber-terrorism offences fit that refined classifica- tion. Sub-section 3.2 presents the case for an extended model which also incorporates contextual information such as main motive/offender role, the offender relationship, and scope of impact, as well as the role of the computer and presents a detailed analy- sis of a number of significant cybercrime case studies using that model to illustrate its expressiveness.

3.1   Refining the Type I/II Classification of Cybercrime

The purpose of reviewing and investigating different definitions and classifications of computer crime is to determine a consistent and comprehensive taxonomy that will benefit the organizations that deal with combating such crimes. Some of the benefits include: sharing of information, accurate reporting of cybercrime cases, cooperation on actual cases, cooperation on combating cybercrime, and harmonization of cyber- crime regulation and legislation. The UN classification of computer crime addresses some main categories of crimes involving computers without considering other types of offences such as copyright and harassment. The CoE computer crime taxonomy is a broader classification. However, the CoE cybercrime classification too does not include a number of other types of crimes that are supported or facilitated using com- puters such as money laundering and identity theft.

We have further below consolidated a comprehensive list of crimes which are gen- erally regarded as cybercrime and classified them according to the Type I and Type II classification. In doing so we have identified different sub-classes for both Type I and Type II offences. These sub-classes appear to us to be intuitive and enable us to arrive at a natural classification of that list of cybercrimes. Some of the previous work on classifying cybercrime reviewed in Section 2 has likewise extended to sub-classes but that work has either by-passed the major Type I/II classification (e.g., CoE [26]), focused solely on computer attacks *per se* (e.g., Kanellis et al [20]), or has merged crimes where the role of the computer is merely incidental to the crime into Type II (e.g., Urbas and Choo [36]). Our sub-classes build on and consolidate some of that previous work to provide a more comprehensive and expressive model. We now describe our refined taxonomy:

Type I crimes include crimes where the computer, computer network, or electronic device is the **target** of the criminal activity. We divide this into four sub-categories:

- Unauthorized access offences [4] such as hacking
- Malicious codes offences [5] such as dissemination of viruses and worms [22]
- Interruption of services offences [24] such as disrupting or denying computer services and applications such as denial of service attacks and Botnets
- Theft or misuse of services [28, 33] such as theft or misuse of someone's Internet account or domain name [24].

Type II crimes include crimes where the computer, computer network, or electronic device is the **tool** used to commit or facilitate the crime. We divide this category into three sub-classes:

- *Content violation offences* [33] such as possession of child pornography, unauthorized possession of military secrets, IP offences
- Unauthorised alteration of data, or software for personal or organisational gain [34] such as online fraud
- Improper use of telecommunications [22] such as cyber stalking, spamming, and the use of carriage service with the intention or conspiracy to commit harmful or criminal activity.

We present this refined taxonomy and a list of common examples of cybercrime classified according to the refined taxonomy in Fig. 1. It is clear that in some of these crimes, the computer plays multiple roles and hence that one crime can be classified under multiple types, however there will typically be one primary role, and hence one primary cybercrime type classification by which to classify the crime. As a result, the categories of Fig. 1 are not necessarily exclusive. This corresponds naturally to the reality that there may actually be several separate offences involved in the one case.

Cyber-terrorism and critical infrastructure attacks pose some interesting issues worthy of further consideration. According to Wilson [25], the U.S. Federal Emergency Management Agency (FEMA) defines 'cyberterrorism' as "unlawful attacks and threats of attack against computers, networks, and the information stored therein when done to intimidate or coerce a government or its people in furtherance of political or social objectives". Coleman [35] defines 'cyberterrorism' as "the premeditated use of disruptive activities, or the threat thereof, against computers and/or networks, with the intention to cause harm or further social, ideological, religious, political or similar objectives, or to intimidate any person in furtherance of such objectives".

According to the UK Parliamentary Office of Science and Technology [36], cyber-criminals may use computers to "damage the functioning of the Critical National Infrastructure (CNI) which includes emergency services, telecommunications, energy distribution and finance, all of which rely on IT". The Australian High Tech Crime Centre [27] categorized cyberterrorism under Type II along with fraud, money laundering and other traditional crimes. Others [25] have considered physical attacks (not using a computer) against critical infrastructure such as Internet, telecommunications, and electric power grid as cyberterrorism.

It seems evident that any attack against a computer and computer network intended for political purposes is a cybercrime and can be labeled as cyberterrorism and Urbas and Choo [28] have indeed categorized cyberterrorism-related offences under Cyber-crime Type I. In fact, any offence that comes under Cybercrime Type I could be considered cyberterrorism if the intent of the attacker is to commit a terrorism act. The FEMA and Coleman definitions of cyberterrorism indicate that some Cybercrime Type II offences can be considered cyberterrorism, depending upon the intent of the attacker (e.g., theft of military secrets). We note therefore that cyber-terrorism may involve offences of both Type I and Type II, for instance, a cyberterrorist needs first to attack a computer or a computer network and misuse computer services in order to get at the power grid. As a result, there are two types of cybercrime in this terrorist act: Type I and Type II.

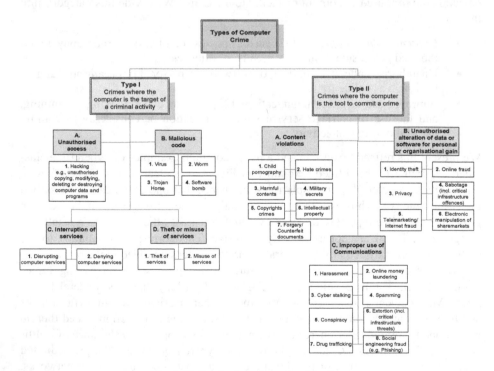

Fig. 1. Refined cybercrime classification

3.2   Extending and Applying the Refined Taxonomy

The question to be asked at this point is how accurately and completely does the above refined classification, illustrated in Fig. 1, depict actual cases of cybercrime? This classification based on identifying the type of the cybercrime and the role/s of the computer in the crime omits to consider some important contextual information such as main motive/offender role, and the offender relationship and scope of impact. Identifying such additional markers promises to be important for government and international bodies who work in the area of crime trends and analysis, and who set strategies to counter and prevent such crimes. We therefore focus in this Sub-section on analysing and investigating some cybercrime cases in more detail, including not just the type of cybercrime in terms of (the refined) Cybercrime Types I and II , but also contextual information regarding main motive/offender role, the offender relationship, and scope of impact. In analysing these cases, we assessed the following characteristics of each offence:

- *The type of cybercrime*: which type or types of cybercrime have been committed (Cybercrime Type I/II)
- *Refined classification*: where does each offence appear in the detailed classification represented in Fig. 1
- *Main motive/offender role*: what are the motives of the offence; is it an individual's motivation, or is it a politically related crime such as information warfare, or terrorism activity, or that of an organized crime group
- *The offender relationship*: how can we classify the offender's relationship to the victim, are they from inside, or outside
- *The scope of impact*: what is the scope of impact of the offence, is the victim or target an individual, business, government agency or global infrastructure such as the Internet.

We have analyzed the following well-known cybercrime case studies according to the refined Type I/II classification scheme and contextual markers identified above:

- Morris worm [37]
- Maroochydore public waterways sewage [38]
- Harassment letter send by email
- U.S. v. Gorshkov & U.S. v. Ivanov [39, 40]
- Fungible credentials [41]
- International Interpol-led investigation on child pornography [42]
- ShadowCrew [43]
- Holiday prize scam [44]
- Fraud and money laundering scheme [45].

Identifying not only the specific nature but also the contextual information of cybercrime in this way is useful to organizations setting strategies and plans to counter cybercrime. We have summarised the results of our analysis in Table 1. Table 1 captures the essential features of the crimes analysed and provides a concise but sufficient description of each crime so as to enable informed reporting and accurate statistical analysis of the nature of the cybercrimes involved. We believe this demonstrates the applicability and utility of the extended refined taxonomy.

4 International Cybercrime Legislation and Compliance with CoE Convention

We focus on the criminal law provisions of the CoE Convention, Articles 2 to 11:

- Articles 2 to 6 in relation to the offences against the confidentiality, integrity and availability of computer data and systems
- Articles 7 and 8 regarding computer related fraud and forgery
- Article 9 concerning content related offences
- Article 10 concerning offences related to infringements of copyright, and
- Article 11 regarding the auxiliary liability and sanctions.

Table 1. Characteristics of some cybercrime case studies

Case #	Case name/detail	Type of computer crime	Refined classification (Fig. 1)	Main motive/offender role	Offender relationship	Scope of Impact
1	Morris worm	Type I	I.B2, I.C1	individual	outsider	Business, government and the Internet
2	Maroochydore public waterways sewage	Type I	I.A1	individual	outsider	Business and government
3	Harassment letter send by email	Type II	II.C1	individual	outsider	individual
4	U.S. v. Gorshkov U.S. v. Ivanov	Type I and Type II	I.A1, II.B2, II.C5, II.C6,	Individuals and organised crime	outsider	business
5	Fungible credentials	Type II	II.A7	Individuals and organised crime	outsider	individuals
6	International Interpol-led investigation on child pornography	Type II	II.A1	Individuals and organised crime	outsider	individuals
7	Shadowcrew	Type I and Type II	I.A1, I.D1, II.B1, II.B2, II.C8	Organised crime	outsider	Individuals and business
8	Holiday prize scam	Type II	II.B2, II.C8	Organised crime	outsider	Individuals
9	Fraud and money laundering scheme	Type II	II.B2, II.C2, II.C5	Organised crime	outsider	Individuals

Source: Markoff [37], Wyld [38], CIO Asia [39], Attfield [40], Berghel [41], Ninemsn [42], Grow & Bush [43], SCAMwatch [44] and the U.S. Department of Justice [45].

In this section we provide a comparative review of the computer crime and cyber-crime legislation used in Australia, the UAE, the UK and the USA in the context of the CoE Convention. It compares the federal computer crime and cybercrime legislation of Australia, the UAE, the UK and the USA, and in particular determines whether and to what extent each of these jurisdictions corresponds to the criminal provisions provided by the CoE Convention, Articles 2 to 11. This section aims to identify the existence of legislation in these four countries that corresponds to the CoE Convention. It also comprises a comparative review of cybercrime legislation enacted in Australia, the UAE, the UK and the USA that aligns with the criminal provisions provided by the CoE Convention.

The findings show that Australia, the UAE, the UK and the USA have federal legislation that covers all the CoE Convention Articles 2 to 11, and the UAE covers all but one – Article 6. We observe also:

- While these four countries have provisions on criminalising offences identified under Articles 2 to11, not all of these offences are criminalised under the one legislation, but rather under different legislations
- With regard to criminal sanctions, all of the four countries provide provisions for the punishment of committing the CoE Convention related offences but that there are some variations in the penalties for committing computer-related offences in these four countries. The USA legislation has provision for longer and tougher penalties. In contrast to the UAE, the UK and the USA, committing one of the computer offences in Australia is more likely to be punished with only an imprisonment term. Also, the UAE criminal sanctions system has smaller and lighter punishments compared to the other countries.

Table 2 lists the cybercrime provisions in Australia, the UAE, the UK and the USA corresponding to the CoE Articles. Additionally, Table 3 illustrates the penalties for committing these offences in Australia, the UAE, the UK and the USA.

In a further step, we investigated the degree of alignment of the legislation with the Articles as presented in Table 4. This is a preliminary evaluation only, a detailed and comprehensive evaluation is outside of the scope of this work and a subject for further work. Each Article 2 to 11 of the CoE Convention has essential criteria such as that the crime must be committed 'intentionally' and 'without right'. In reviewing the legislation we assessed it against these essential criteria. Table 4 shows the results of the preliminary analysis. It is apparently the case that the degree of alignment with Articles 2 to 11 of the CoE Convention as represented in Table 4 is low in Australia and the UK and very low in the UAE.

The USA alignment truly reflects its involvement from the beginning in the development of the CoE Convention. Moreover, the USA is one of the countries that have ratified the CoE Convention which came into force in 2006. Nevertheless, other factors may have also contributed to this, including the fact that the Internet itself was started and developed in the USA.

Australia and the UK are largely aligned with Articles 2 to 11 of the CoE Convention. This may correspond clearly to the fact that the Cybercrime Act 2001 of Australia is developed based on the Computer Misuse Act 1990 of the UK. Yet, both Acts focus mainly on making illegal the offences against the confidentiality, integrity and the availability of computer data and systems. Section 477.1 of the Cybercrime Act 2001 of Australia and Section 2 of the Computer Misuse Act 1990 of the UK make illegal the unauthorized use of a computer system to commit any of the offences listed under their legislation. These two sections work as an umbrella to make illegal any misuse of computers, even if it is not directed to damage computer data and systems.

The findings show that the UAE is the country least aligned with the CoE Convention. Certain factors may contribute to this finding. The UAE Federal Law No 2 on the Prevention of Information Technology Crimes was only enacted in 2006. Also, on 16 December 2009, the UAE Minister of Justice, Dr Hadef Al Daheri, noted that the UAE Government was setting up a new Department under their Federal Courts to combat cybercrime [46]. The intention of the department was to draft new laws and regulations concerning cybercrime, and set plans for prevention mechanisms and

Table 2. Summary of Australia, UAE, UK and US legislation corresponding to the CoE Convention

CoE Convention	Australia	UAE	UK	USA
Article 2 - Illegal access	Cybercrime Act 2001, Criminal Code Act 1995 (Cth): Section 478.1	UAE Federal Law No 2 of 2006: Article 2	Computer Misuse Act 1990: Section 1	Computer Fraud and Abuse Act, U.S. Code Title 18 Section 1030 (a) (1) – (5)
Article 3 - Illegal interception	Telecommunications (Interception and Access) Act 1979 (Cth): Subsection 7 (1)	UAE Federal Law No 2 of 2006: Article 8	Regulation of Investigatory Powers Act 2000 (RIPA)	U.S. Code Title 18 Sections 2510-2522, Wire and Electronic Communications Interception and Interception of Oral Communications
Article 4 - Data interference	Cybercrime Act 2001, Criminal Code Act 1995 (Cth): Sections 477.2 and 478.2	UAE Federal Law No 2 of 2006: Articles 2 and 6	Computer Misuse Act 1990: Section 3, Data Protection Act 1998	Computer Fraud and Abuse Act, U.S. Code Title 18 Section 1030 (a)(5)
Article 5 - System interference	Cybercrime Act 2001, Criminal Code Act 1995 (Cth): Sections 477.3 and 474.14	UAE Federal Law No 2 of 2006: Article 5	Computer Misuse Act 1990: Section 3	Computer Fraud and Abuse Act, U.S. Code Title 18 Section 1030 (a)(5)
Article 6 - Misuse of devices	Cybercrime Act 2001, Criminal Code Act 1995 (Cth): Sections 478.3 and 478.4		Computer Misuse Act 1990: Section 3A	Computer Fraud and Abuse Act, U.S. Code Title 18 Sections 1029, 1030 (a)(5)(A) and 2512
Article 7 - Computer-related forgery	Criminal Code Act 1995 (Cth): Div 144, Div 145 and Div 477: Section 477.1	UAE Federal Law No 2 of 2006: Articles 4, 7 and 10	Computer Misuse Act 1990: Section 2, Forgery and Counterfeiting Act 1981	Computer Fraud and Abuse Act, U.S. Code Title 18 Sections 1029, 1037 and 1028, Chapter 25
Article 8 - Computer-related fraud	Criminal Code Act 1995 (Cth): Div 134, Div 135, and Div 477: Section 477.1	UAE Federal Law No 2 of 2006: Articles 10 and 11	Computer Misuse Act 1990: Section 2, Fraud Act 2006: Sections 6 and 7	Computer Fraud and Abuse Act, U.S. Code Title 18 Sections 1029, 1030 (a)(4) and 1343
Article 9 - Offences related to child pornography	Criminal Code Act 1995 (Cth): Sections 474.19 and 474.20, Customs Act 1901 (Cth): Section 233BAB	UAE Federal Law No 2 of 2006: Articles 12 and 13	Protection of Children Act 1978, Sexual Offenses Act 2003, Criminal Justice Act 1988: Sections 160 and 161	Sexual Exploitation of Children, U.S. Code Title 18 Sections 2251, 2252 and 2252A
Article 10 - Offences related to infringements of copyright and related rights	Copyright Act 1968 (Cth)	UAE Federal Law No 7 of 2002 regarding Copyright and Related Rights	Copyright, Design and Patents Act 1988	U.S. Code Title 18 Section 2319, 1030, and 1029 and Title 17: Section 506
Article 11 - Attempt and adding or abetting	Criminal Code Act 1995 (Cth): Sections 478.3 and 478.4	UAE Federal Law No 2 of 2006: Article 23	Computer Misuse Act 1990: Section 2	U.S. Code Title 18 Section 1030 (b)

Table 3. Comparison of penalties[2] for committing computer-related offences identified by the CoE Convention

CoE Convention	Australia	UAE	UK	USA
Article 2 - Illegal access	two years imprisonment	fine and/or at least one year imprisonment	fine and/or up to two years imprisonment	fine and/or up to two years imprisonment
Article 3 - Illegal interception	two years imprisonment	fine and/or imprisonment	fine and/or up to two years imprisonment	fine and/or up to five years imprisonment
Article 4 - Data interference	imprisonment for up to ten years (under s. 477.2)	fine and/or imprisonment	fine and/or up to ten years imprisonment	fine and/or up to ten years imprisonment
Article 5 - System interference	ten years imprisonment	fine and/or imprisonment	fine and/or up to ten years imprisonment	fine and/or up to ten years imprisonment
Article 6 - Misuse of devices	three years imprisonment (under s. 478.4)		fine and/or up to two years imprisonment	fine and/or up to five years imprisonment
Article 7 - Computer-related forgery	imprisonment for up to ten years (under Div 145)	fine and/or at least one year imprisonment	up to five years imprisonment	fine and/or up to fifteen years imprisonment
Article 8 - Computer-related fraud	imprisonment for up to ten years	fine and/or at least one year imprisonment	fine and/or up to ten years imprisonment	fine and/or up to twenty years imprisonment
Article 9 - Offences related to child pornography	imprisonment for up to ten years (under s. 474.19 or s. 474.20)	fine and/or at least five years imprisonment	Imprisonment for up to fourteen years	fine and/or up to thirty years imprisonment
Article 10 - Offences related to infringements of copyright and related rights	fine and/or imprisonment	fine and/or imprisonment	fine and/or up to ten years imprisonment	fine and/or up to ten years imprisonment
Article 11 - Attempt and adding or abetting	three years imprisonment (under s. 478.3 and s. 478.4)	fine and/or imprisonment	fine and/or imprisonment	fine and/or imprisonment

---

[2] The penalties here depend mainly on violating one section or article of the computer crime or cybercrime law, and accordingly, it could be vary and higher if the committed offence was a second or third offence, not the first committed offence of this type. For instance, violating section 1030 (a)(5) of the U.S. Code is punished by a fine and/or a maximum of ten years imprisonment if it was as a first offence, but if it was as a second offence, the punishment could be up to twenty years imprisonment.

Table 4. Alignment with the CoE Provisions

CoE Convention	Australia	UAE	UK	USA
Article 2 – Illegal access	√	√	√	√
Article 3 – Illegal interception				√
Article 4 – Data interference	√	√	√	√
Article 5 – System interference	√		√	√
Article 6 – Misuse of Devices				√
Article 7 – Computer-related forgery	√		√	√
Article 8 – Computer-related fraud				√
Article 9 – Offences related to child pornography	√	√	√	√
Article 10 – Offences related to infringements of copyright and related rights	√	√	√	√
Article 11 – Attempt and adding or abetting	√		√	√

coordination with law enforcement agencies. Also, we need to consider that cultural factors are an important determinant of a country's regulations. The UAE culture is in many ways significantly different from the culture in Australia, the UK and the USA, as we determined in a separate work addressing cultural influences on national anti-money laundering legislation [47].

Furthermore, our findings indicate that one of the main reasons behind the UAE low alignment with the CoE Convention is the lack of some important conditions for the offences listed under its Law. Most of the UAE Articles do not require the offence to be committed intentionally and without right. These are two important conditions, especially when dealing with cybercrime. While it is not difficult to prove that an offence is committed without right, it is, in practice, difficult and challenging to confirm that the offence was committed intentionally. Articles 2 to11 of the CoE Convention require the offence to be committed 'intentionally', 'wilfully', in Article 10, for criminal liability to apply. Therefore, there is a need to understand the importance of inserting the condition 'intentionally' within the legislation, something which in principle will therefore allow the 'Trojan Horse' defence.

In summary, the above indicates that the UAE legislation is required to be updated. This is but one example of argument in support of the International Telecommunication Union (ITU) 2009 plea for international harmonization [48]: "The lack of a globally harmonized legal framework with respect to cyber criminal activities has become an issue requiring the urgent attention of all nations". While there has been some progress on the legislative front, most notably as a result of the CoE Convention, nonetheless as recently as April 2010 we see a proposal for a global cybercrime treaty rejected at the UN. It seems very clear that there is a need for progress on this front and that to have a global convention on cybercrime, the UN, as an international organization, should take a main role in such a convention and that the CoE Convention which has identified a comprehensive set of computer offences, should be used as a starting point. We argue that this aim must be pursued and that to assist in achieving the aim a six step strategy is required, involving and based on regional participation (this is reminiscent of how Financial Action Task Force (FATF)[3] regional bodies have

---

[3] The FATF was established in 1989 by the G7 in response to increased concern about money laundering. It develops and promotes policies on AML/CFT; and examines and evaluates its members' AML/CFT approaches (http://www.fatf-gafi.org).

cooperated with the international FATF to achieve anti-money laundering/combating financing of terrorism (AML/CFT) aims [40]):

1. identify the main player (the UN) and contributing international organizations (e,g., ITU, CoE, Interpol, G8)
2. identify the sub-players world-wide (regional bodies)
3. identify the relationships between the various participants
4. develop timetables for regional bodies to negotiate and report back to UN on CoE and ITU cybercrime initiatives
5. develop timetables for contributing international organizations to negotiate and report back on CoE and ITU initiatives
6. reconciliation at UN level followed by further cycles of reporting and feedback between participating bodies (essentially re-iteration of steps iv/, v/ and vi/)

5 Australia and the UAE - The Fight against Cybercrime

As part of our studies into how the fight against cybercrime is proceeding internationally, we have analysed the law enforcement procedures employed to combat computer crime, and the legal context in which this occurs, in the state of Queensland in Australia and in the Emirate of Abu Dhabi in the UAE. We have studied the approaches used by the Queensland Police Service (QPS) in Australia and by the Abu Dhabi Police service (ADP) in the UAE to fight cybercrime.

There are two reasons for choosing the ADP to participate in this research project. Firstly, the ADP is funding the project and secondly, the researcher has approval to access and conduct this research in ADP. There are also two reasons for choosing QPS to participate in this research project. Firstly, the research project is located in Queensland and secondly, the researcher, through the cooperation between the QPS and the ADP, has approval to conduct this research. Additionally, we had obtained ethics clearance from the Queensland University of Technology ethics committee to conduct this research.

In order to achieve the objectives, we were given access by the respective law enforcement agencies to some relevant departmental sections. Because of the unavailability of documented procedures on how computer crime units in either the QPS or the ADP operate, identifying their procedures has been achieved through the use of questionnaires completed by the officers and by face to face interviews. Analysis of the resulting data focuses in particular on how the procedures and approaches to combat computer crime by these two law enforcement agencies differ and what improvements are predicated and the nature of the implications for combating computer crime internationally.

Investigating the nature of procedures and guidelines employed by the two agencies using written questionnaires and face to face interviews with the relevant officers has the benefit that it casts light also on the degree to which there is a consistent awareness and interpretation of procedures and guidelines. The study has been conducted in two phases, Phase I and Phase II. Phase I of the study was a pilot study which used a written questionnaire followed by interviews conducted with officers of the two police services, QPS and ADP. The written questionnaire was developed based on the literature review and previous informal meetings with officers from QPS. The Phase I questionnaire questions were developed and structured into three different categories. These categories are:

- Legislation and jurisdiction
- Policy, procedures and resources
- The nature and extent of cybercrime.

Additionally, the second category of *policy, procedures and resources*, included the following themes: policy and procedures; investigation processes; officer experience; resources - technology and computer forensics resources; time to investigate computer crime; education and training; and reporting and statistics.

Then, after analyzing the questionnaire responses, we developed the follow-up interview questions. The questionnaire and interviews were designed to identify how the two law enforcement agencies investigate computer crime, their awareness of the relevant legislation, and their awareness of agency procedures and guidelines for investigating computer-related crime. Phase I found that responses in some areas required further clarification due to issues of unclear and inconsistent responses.

Phase II included performing follow-up in-depth studies using a second written questionnaire and a second set of interviews. This second questionnaire was developed based on the results of Phase I and in line with the research objective. It intended to clarify several responses in some areas that required further clarification due to issues of unclear and inconsistent responses. It also intended to answer additional questions related to computer crime such as jurisdictions, statistics and search warrants.

Our analysis of the data we obtained shows that the ADP and QPS approaches have a number of similar challenges and issues. There are some important issues that continue to create problems for the law enforcement agencies such as sufficient resources, coping internationally with computer crime legislation that differs between countries, and cooperation and communication problems between countries.

This study has also highlighted the importance of having comprehensive documented procedures and guidelines for combating cybercrime. There is a need for formal policy, procedures and guidelines documents regarding the investigation of computer crime. The study also highlights the importance of providing education and training for staff to keep them updated with emerging forms of crime. In summary, we identified the following areas where improvement is mainly needed:

1. availability of formal policy, procedures and guidelines documents
2. resourcing in terms of personnel
3. reporting and recording of cybercrime as distinct from other forms of crime.

6 Conclusions and Future Work

As mentioned earlier, the ITU (2009) notes: "The lack of a globally harmonized legal framework with respect to cyber criminal activities has become an issue requiring the urgent attention of all nations". This may underestimate the criticality of the problem. Since WW II the world has faced a number of critical global problems. Starvation and genocide, the threat of nuclear war, and - more recently - terrorism, the global financial crisis, and climate change. These problems have required nations around the world to cooperate in pursuit of the common good. The world must recognize that cybercrime is potentially a problem whose seriousness is comparable to that of some of the above given the reliance of government and industry and commerce on the Internet. Indeed, cybercrime clearly contributes to and makes worse some of those problems, something recognized by the FATF whose efforts have been described earlier. Through the Internet we have created a virtual world that is universally accessible and transnational. It is as a result regulated in a largely ad hoc manner which makes it a rich environment for criminal behaviour. We have created this international virtual world for our convenience but have neglected to design and implement its proper governance. Our paper describes work we have done which we believe can in a small way assist in developing that governance.

We have investigated and analysed some of the issues surrounding disparate definitions and taxonomies of cybercrime and developed a refined and extended taxonomy of cybercrime based upon the dual characteristics of the role of the computer and the contextual nature of the crime. We have used this refined extended taxonomy to analyse a number of iconic cybercrime cases in order to demonstrate its applicability and propose its adoption internationally. We have explored the influence of the CoE Convention internationally by analyzing how the USA, the UK, Australia and the UAE conform to the Convention. These four countries represent a spectrum of development and culture and our results show not surprisingly that more needs to be done in order to address the issue identified by the ITU. We believe a regional approach as we describe in Section 4 is required to progress activities on this front. As part of our analysis of how the fight against cybercrime is proceeding globally, the paper concludes with a comparison of the approaches used by the QPS in Australia and by the ADP in the UAE to fight cybercrime. The analysis shows that resourcing is a problem, and so too are the availability of formal policy, procedures and guidelines documents and the reporting of cybercrime.

Two directions we believe need to be pursued in addition to the above are the detailed evaluation of conformance of national cybercrime legislation with the CoE Convention on Cybercrime, and further research into the comprehensive reporting of cybercrime at the national level in order to provide regulators and legislators with accurate information on cybercrime trends. The reporting needs to include data regarding all cases, regardless of courtroom outcome, together with the extent of resources involved.

References

1. Grabosky, P., Smith, R.G., Dempsey, G.: Electronic Theft: Unlawful Acquisition in Cyberspace. Cambridge University Press, Cambridge (2001)
2. Grabosky, P.: The Global and Regional Cyber Crime Problem. In: Broadhurst, R.G. (ed.) Proceedings of the Asia Cyber Crime Summit, pp. 22–42. Centre for Criminology, The University of Hong Kong, Hong Kong (2001)
3. Furnell, S.M.: The Problem of Categorising Cybercrime and Cybercriminals. In: 2nd Australian Information Warfare and Security Conference, Perth, Australia, pp. 29–36 (2001)
4. United Nations (UN). International Review of Criminal Policy - United Nations manual on the prevention and control of computer-related crime (1999),
   http://www.uncjin.org/8th.pdf (cited December 6, 2006)
5. G8 Government/Industry Conference on High-Tech Crime. Report of Workshop 3: Threat assessment and prevention. G8 Government/Industry Conference on High-Tech Crime (2001),
   http://www.mofa.go.jp/policy/i_crime/high_tec/
   conf0105-6.html (cited March 6, 2007)

6. Krone, T.: High Tech Crime Brief: Concepts and terms (2005), http://www.aic.gov.au/publications/htcb/htcb001.pdf (cited February 1, 2007)

7. Kelly, J.X.: Cybercrime - High tech crime (2002), http://www.jisclegal.ac.uk/cybercrime/Archived_cybercrime.htm (cited March 1, 2007)

8. Gordon, S., Ford, R.: On the Definition and Classification of Cybercrime. Journal of Computer Virology 2(1), 13–20 (2006)

9. Broadhurst, R., Grabosky, P. (eds.): Cyber-crime: The challenge in Asia, p. 434. Hong Kong University Press, Hong Kong (2005)

10. Smith, R.G., Grabosky, P., Urbas, G.: Cyber Criminals on Trial, p. 262. Cambridge University Press, Melbourne (2004)

11. Pokar, F.: New Challenges for International Rules Against Cyber-crime. European Journal on Criminal Policy and Research 10(1), 27–37 (2004)

12. Foreign Affairs and International Trade Canada. Cyber Crime, August 16 (2004), http://www.dfait-maeci.gc.ca/internationalcrime/cybercrime-en.asp (cited December 5, 2006)

13. Cybercitizenship. What is Cyber Crime? (2008), http://cybercitizenship.org/crime/crime.html (cited February 19, 2008)

14. Symantec Corporation. What is Cybercrime? (2007), http://www.symantec.com/avcenter/cybercrime/index_page2.html (cited February 5, 2007)

15. Kshetri, N.: The Simple Economics of Cybercrimes. IEEE Security & Privacy 4(1), 33–39 (2006)

16. Wall, D.S.: Cybercrimes: New wine, no bottles? In: Davies, P., Francis, P., Jupp, V. (eds.) Invisible Crimes: Their Victims and their Regulation. Macmillan, London (1999)

17. Grabosky, P.N.: Virtual Criminality: Old Wine in New Bottles? Social & Legal Studies 10(2), 243–249 (2001)

18. Council of Europe. Convention on Cybercrime (2001), http://conventions.coe.int/Treaty/EN/Treaties/Html/185.htm (cited February 10, 2009)

19. Computer Crime and Intellectual Property Section Criminal Division at U.S. Department of Justice. Prosecuting computer crimes (2007)

20. UK Metropolitan Police Service (MPS). Progress of MPS E-crime Strategy (2007), http://www.mpa.gov.uk/print/committees/mpa/2007/070125/10.htm (cited January 10, 2008)

21. Secretariat of the Parliamentary Joint Committee on the Australian Crime Commission. Cybercrime (2004), http://www.aph.gov.au/senate/committee/acc_ctte/completed_inquiries/2002-04/cybercrime/report/report.pdf (cited January 15, 2008)

22. Brenner, S.W.: U.S. Cybercrime Law: Defining offences. Information Systems Frontiers 6(2), 115–132 (2004)

23. Sukhai, N.B.: Hacking and Cybercrime. In: Proceedings of the 1st Annual Conference on Information Security Curriculum Development, I.s.c. development, Editor, pp. 128–132. ACM Press, Kennesaw (2004)

24. Koenig, D.: Investigation of Cybercrime and Technology-related Crime (2002), http://www.neiassociates.org/cybercrime.htm (cited June 25, 2008)

25. Wilson, C.: Botnets, Cybercrime, and Cyberterrorism: Vulnerabilities and policy issues for congress (2008), http://fas.org/sgp/crs/terror/RL32114.pdf (cited June 26, 2008)
26. Lewis, B.C.: Preventing of Computer Crime Amidst International Anarchy (2004), http://goliath.ecnext.com/coms2/summary_0199-3456285_ITM (cited November 17, 2008)
27. Australian High Tech Crime Centre (AHTCC): Fighting the Invisible. Platypus Magazine: Journal of the Australian Federal Police 80, 4–6 (2003), http://www.afp.gov.au/~/media/afp/pdf/f/fighting-the-invisible.ashx
28. Urbas, G., Choo, K.-K.R.: Resources Materials on Technology-enabled Crime, No. 28 (2008), http://www.aic.gov.au/publications/tbp/tbp028/tbp028.pdf (cited November 16, 2008)
29. Thomas, D.: An Uncertain World. The British Computer Society 48(5), 12–13 (2006)
30. Kanellis, P., et al. (eds.): Digital Crime and Forensic Science in Cyberspace. Idea Group Inc., London (2006)
31. Chakrabarti, A., Manimaran, G.: Internet Infrastructure Security: A taxonomy. IEEE Network 16(6), 13–21 (2002)
32. Krone, T.: High Tech Crime Brief: Hacking motives (2005), http://www.aic.gov.au/publications/htcb/htcb006.html (cited February 12, 2007)
33. Keyser, M.: The Council of Europe Convention on Cybercrime. Transnational Law and Policy Journal 12(2), 287–326 (2003)
34. Brenner, S.W.: Defining Cybercrime: A review of the state and federal law. In: Clifford, R.D. (ed.) Cybercrime: The Investigation, Prosecution and Defence of a Computer-Related Crime, pp. 12–40. Carolina Academic Press, North Carolina (2006)
35. Coleman, K.: Cyber Terrorism (2003), http://www.directionsmag.com/article.php?article_id=432&trv=1 (cited February 10, 2009)
36. The UK Parliament Office of Science and Technology. Computer crime (2006), http://www.parliament.uk/documents/upload/postpn271.pdf (cited March 1, 2007)
37. Markoff, J.: Computer Intruder is put on Probation and Fined $10,000 (1990), http://query.nytimes.com/gst/fullpage.html?res=9C0CE1D71038F936A35756C0A966958260 (cited October 7, 2008)
38. Wyld, B.: Cyberterrorism: Fear factor (2004), http://www.crime-research.org/analytics/501/ (cited October 7, 2008)
39. CIO Asia. A Hacker Story (2005), http://www.crime-research.org/articles/hacker0405/ (cited May 28, 2008)
40. Attfield, P.: United States v Gorshkov Detailed Forensics and Case Study: Expert witness perspective, pp. 3–24. IEEE Computer Society, Los Alamitos (2005)
41. Berghel, H.: Fungible Credentials and Next-generation Fraud. Communications of the ACM 49(12), 15–19 (2006)
42. Ninemsn. Cop's Child Porn Case Delayed to Friday (2008), http://news.ninemsn.com.au/article.aspx?id=575167 (cited June 6, 2008)

43. Grow, B., Bush, J.: Hacker Hunters (2005),
    http://www.businessweek.com/magazine/content/
    05_22/b3935001_mz001.htm (cited October 21, 2006)
44. SCAMwatch. The Holiday Prize Which Nearly Cost Nicole Thousands of Dollars (2008),
    http://www.scamwatch.gov.au/content/index.phtml/itemId/699124
    (cited October 17, 2008)
45. U.S. Department of Justice. Fourth defendant in massive Internet scam pleads guilty to
    fraud and money laundering charges (2004),
    http://www.usdoj.gov/criminal/cybercrime/
    nordickPlea_triwest.htm (cited November 3, 2008)
46. Gulfnews. New Department to Fight Cyber Crimes (2009),
    http://gulfnews.com/news/gulf/uae/crime/
    new-department-to-fight-cyber-crimes-1.554070
    (cited December 25, 2009)
47. Alkaabi, A., et al.: A Comparative Analysis of the Extent of Money Laundering in Austra-
    lia, UAE, UK and the USA. In: Finance and Corporate Governance Conference, Mel-
    bourne (2010), http://ssrn.com/abstract=1539843
48. International Telecommunication Union. ITU Toolkit for Cybercrime Legislation (2009)
    (updated on February 2010),
    http://www.itu.int/ITU-D/cyb/cybersecurity/docs/
    itu-toolkit-cybercrime-legislation.pdf (cited November 3, 2009)

Software Piracy Forensics: The Need for Further Developing AFC

S. Santhosh Baboo[1] and P. Vinod Bhattathiripad[2,*]

[1] Reader, P G & Research Dept. of Computer Science, D.G. Vasihanv College, Chennai, India
santhos2001@sify.com
[2] Consulting Cyber Forensic Engineer, Calicut, Kerala, India
vinodpolpaya@gmail.com

Abstract. Among all the available approaches for software piracy forensics, one existing and exceptional approach is the theoretical frame work called AFC (Abstraction-Filtering-Comparison), an accepted approach in US courts for evaluating copyright infringement claims involving computer software. Through this paper, the authors would like to approach AFC in a threefold manner: One, to discuss the nature and efficacy of AFC; two, to recount some existing observations on it, and three, to identify areas, if any, where there is scope and need for appropriate modifications to further increase the efficacy and validate the legitimacy of the AFC approach, and in particular from the view point of a researcher who believes that software intelligence offered by the automated tools for software piracy investigation needs to be supplemented with manual intelligence for making the expert report more judiciary-friendly.

Keywords: Piracy, Post-piracy modifications, Copyright infringement, Software piracy forensics, AFC, MIS forensics, Abstraction-Filtration-Comparison, Nuggets, Computer Associates vs. Altai case, Scènes a faire.

1 Introduction

In any court case, the technical expert's evidence is open to legal challenge and such challenges, irrespective of the outcome, might delay the process of litigation. Hence, it is both crucial and necessary for the expert's report to be as thorough, authentic and convincing as possible in the interest of proper justice. Also, it is important for the expert to preempt any delay by making the report as comprehensive and complete as possible. This is all the more important in software piracy litigation where a cyber forensic expert (technical expert) is the person who is often designated by the judge to compare the pirated[1] with the original[2] and prepare a report that is legally convincing and binding. Although software tools are available to help them to carry out this cyber forensic assignment, the experts need to supplement the software intelligence with

---

* Research Scholar, Bharathiar University, Coimbatore.
[1] Throughout this article, pirated means the allegedly pirated software.
[2] Throughout this article, original means the version of the software that the complainant submits to the law enforcement agency for software piracy forensics.

I. Baggili (Ed.): ICDF2C 2010, LNICST 53, pp. 19–26, 2011.

human intelligence, insight and common sense so as to produce and present a report as unchallengeable as possible[3].

The natural modus operandi of the expert is to compare the original and pirated software by juxtaposing the two [1]. The task of comparing two software packages arises usually when one party lodges a complaint of software piracy against another. In order to perform this task, several software tools are used to assess software piracy and these tools are based mostly on academically accepted mathematical techniques and theoretical frameworks like Discourse Analysis [2], SMAT [3], MOSS [4], IDENTIFIED [5], SCAP [5,6], and AFC [7]. All these tools are capable in their respective areas of software piracy investigation but the inherent complexity in software programming logic and underlying global commonalities in it demand a vital supplementing role for cyber forensic expert's intelligence, expertise, common sense, insight and perhaps even intuition. So, even if there are automated approaches to software comparison, there is still scope and space for a comprehensive approach (for manually comparing two software packages), which utilizes the expert's intelligence, expertise, common sense and insight. While it is true that automated comparison ensures certain level of consistency, reliability and thus, integrity of the result, manual comparison, which supplements and not replaces automated comparison, would give the expert scope to add value to the result. Such a value added report could be useful to the judge.

A manual approach of comparing two software packages needs to address comparison issues related to various parts of the software like source code, object code, databases, and fingerprints. Source code and object code comparisons need to be performed along various sub-parts (of source code, object code, databases, and fingerprints) like data structures, algorithms, system calls, errors, language, formatting, macros, comment styles, spelling, grammar, use of language features, execution paths, bugs and metrics [8]. All these areas of comparison provide enough challenge for the software piracy forensics researcher who works with the objective of formulating a methodology for manually comparing two software packages for adding value to the automated result of the same comparison.

Any such researcher cannot stay away from recounting AFC (Abstraction-Filtering-Comparison) because of AFC's judicial acceptance as a manual approach. AFC test was primarily developed by Randall Davis of the Massachusetts Institute of Technology for evaluating copyright infringement claims involving computer software and used in the 1992 Computer Associates vs. Altai case, in the court of appeal of the 2nd federal circuit in the United States [7]. Since 1992, AFC has been recognized as a legal precedent for evaluating copyright infringement claims involving computer software in several appeal courts in the United States, including the fourth, tenth, eleventh and federal circuit courts of appeals [9,10,11]. Even though AFC is basically a manual comparison approach, there exists software tool by name SIMILE workshop, which was developed based on AFC's theoretical frame work in 2007 by the French firm, European Software Analysis Laboratory (EsaLab) with additional inputs from Institut d''electronique et d'informatique Gaspard-Monge – IGM, University of Marne-la-Vall´ee, France [9]. EsaLab claims that SIMILE Workshop is the only software tool (available in the market) based on AFC [9]. All these confirm

---

[3] Our sincere gratitude to the reviewers of this paper for their valuable suggestions.

AFC's fitness both as a manual approach and as a theoretical foundation for a software tool for establishing copyright infringement claims involving computer software and so, any researcher (who works with the objective of formulating an advanced methodology for manually comparing two software packages) cannot avoid AFC.

The main objective of this paper is basically threefold[4]: One, to discuss the nature and efficacy of AFC; two, to recount some existing observations on it, and three, to identify areas, if any, where there is scope and need for appropriate modifications to further increase the efficacy and validate the legitimacy of the AFC approach, and in particular from the view point of a researcher who believes that software intelligence offered by the automated tools for software piracy investigation needs to be supplemented with manual intelligence for making the expert report more judiciary-friendly.

2 The AFC Test

The theoretical framework of AFC not only makes possible the determination of "literal" similarities between two pieces of code, but it also takes into account their functionality to identify "substantial" similarities [9]. In the AFC test, both the pirated as well as the original software are put through three stages, namely, abstraction, filtration and comparison. While other approaches (and the automated tools based on these approaches) generally compare two software packages literally, without considering globally common elements in the software, AFC, as the name indicates, first abstracts the original as well as the allegedly pirated, then filters out the globally common elements in them to zero in on two sets of comparable elements and finally compares these two sets to bring out similarities or "nuggets" [9].

The task of 'abstracting' software is not very easy to perform. In the 1992 *Computer Associates v. Altai* case [12], the abstraction was described according to the following 6 levels: (i) main purpose of the code, (ii) program structure or architecture, (iii) modules, (iv) algorithms and data structures, (v) source codes, (vi) object codes. "At the lowest level of abstraction, a computer program may be thought of in its entirety as a set of individual instructions organized into a hierarchy of modules. At a higher level of abstraction, the instructions in the lowest- level modules may be replaced conceptually by the functions of those modules. At progressively higher levels of abstraction, the functions of higher-level modules conceptually replace the implementations of those modules in terms of lower-level modules and instructions, until finally, one is left with nothing but the ultimate function of the program.... A program has structure at every level of abstraction at which it is viewed. At low levels of abstraction, a program's structure may be quite complex; at the highest level it is trivial" [12, p.13]. That means, in the absence of specific standard procedure, abstraction of hundreds of thousands (sometimes even millions of) lines of codes, presented with high degree of complexity, is a "prodigious undertaking" [13, p.4], even for a computer professional.

Just as abstraction, the task of filtering out the variety of globally shared (and hence non-protectable) expressions generally found in any software is also not an easy task. The AFC-test specifies three categories (more aptly, levels) of exclusions,

---

[4] Our sincere gratitude to Dr. P.B. Nayar, Lincoln University, UK, for his help in articulating our thoughts.

called doctrines [9]. Firstly, if there is only one way of effectively expressing an idea (a function), this idea and its expression tend to "merge". Since the idea itself would not be protectable, the expression of this idea would also escape from the field of the protection. Secondly, there is the "scènes a faire" doctrine which excludes from the field of protection, any code that has been made necessary by the technical environment or some external rules imposed on the programmer. Thirdly, there are those elements that are in the public domain. Thus, carrying out the task of filtration is also not very easy unless there is a standard procedure to filter out the variety of globally shared expressions generally found in any software and thus to zero in on the software elements that form the basis for the software piracy investigation.

Infallibility of AFC. The infallibility of the AFC approach has not stayed unquestioned. One of the best observations on AFC is the amicus brief [13] submitted to the United States court of appeals for the second circuit. This amicus brief was filed in 1996 by Mark M. Arkin, Counsel on behalf of five computer scientists, Roy Campbell (University of Illinois), Lee A. Hollaar (University of Utah), Randall Davis (the inventor of AFC), Gerald J. Sussman, and Hal Abelson, (all three of Massachusetts Institute of Technology), who believed that there was uncertainty among courts in how to implement the AFC for evaluating copyright infringement claims involving computer software. This legal document describes the technical complexity and difficulty of performing the AFC test "from the standpoint of computer science", which these five computer scientists have experienced in their role as experts. The amicus brief observes that "Performing AFC test in the context of litigation is a challenging task, in no small measure because of the technical difficulties that arise. These technical difficulties stem from (1) the sheer magnitude of the task of analyzing programs that routinely consist of hundreds of thousands of lines of computer code, (2) the lack of any fixed or agreed-upon set of levels of abstraction by which to describe a program, (3) the interaction of legal doctrines (such as merger, scenes a faire, and public domain) with the technical constraints of the computer industry and (4) the rapid evolution of these doctrines in the areas of computer software" [13, p. 4]. Lee A. Hollaar, in a later work [14], has further emphasized the supplementary role of the expert's insight and commonsense in the interpretation of the AFC. Our principal contention here is that this need should be looked at more carefully by upgrading its status from supplementarity to essentiality. The expert's input is also vital in the further development and modification of AFC.

The amicus brief further observes that the filtration process also requires substantial technical expertise both to draw a line between idea and expression and to determine whether the expression in a body of code is necessarily incidental to the idea being expressed (merger). To make matters worse, most of the abstractions used to describe the software may not qualify for final comparison (that means, most of them get filtered out in the filtration stage) as most software, especially those for commercial purpose, are written using well-known ideas, designs and principles, because the known (well-tested) design principles are globally believed to be most reliable [13]. Even then, the amicus brief suggests that "despite the difficulty of the task, creating a set of abstractions and answering the technical questions raised in the filtration are still sensible and well-founded undertakings" [13, p. 6] and the task of abstraction should be necessarily carried out based on the control structure, data structures, data flow, information architecture and the textual organization of the code. Finally, this amicus brief suggests legal and technical procedures for applying the AFC test by courts in copyright claims involving software. While the suggested legal procedure may well be comprehensive and practical, the suggested technical procedure seems to be not capable enough to reduce the difficulty of abstraction and filtration and this difficulty remains as a limitation of AFC, even now. Even with this limitation, AFC continued to be an acceptable approach for US courts for comparing the original with the pirated and had been used in several subsequent suits on copyright infringement and trade secret misappropriation involving software [9].

Another observation (on AFC) worth mentioning is the one by honorable judge John M. Walker, Jr., through his article "Protectable 'Nuggets': Drawing the line between idea and expression in computer program copyright protection" [7]. Through this article, the judge explains the difficulties in drawing the line between the idea and expression in software. By observing that the group of three doctrines (listed above) "is not exclusive" and that "one might expect in future cases to see filtration occurring with respect to other program elements, including those listed in § 102(b) of the copyright act, such as procedures, process and methods of operation", the judge fears that "even under an expanded list of elements excluded by the filtration step, there could still be many "nuggets" of protectable expression left in a program" [7, p.83] and because of this, the filtration stage is a battleground where the attorney who is able to argue successfully that his client's program, after filtration, contains many elements of protected expression should be all the more likely to succeed on a claim of infringement. These observations of the judge also point to the limitation of the filtration stage.

Baboo and Bhattathiripad [1][15] explore an interesting point of how to deal with the increasing use of design patterns and programming patterns in general software piracy forensics. This is applicable to AFC too. While this presumably comes under some of the "doctrine" exceptions, to date it does not seem to have been explicitly examined. This is further discussed below, in the context of the limitations of AFC.

Firstly, AFC does not recognize or uphold the need to identify and filter out post-piracy modifications in original as well as in the allegedly pirated. There is a serious risk of the expert's opinion being challenged in the court if post-piracy modifications are not properly identified and filtered out of both original as well as allegedly pirated, before comparing these two [1]. During the post-piracy life span of the software, the original and pirated software are expected to grow functionally almost in the same direction but with stylistically different patterns. The possibility of different patterns of growth is a very valuable and useful dimension of study for the software piracy forensic expert. A proper manual investigation into the potential post-piracy modifications in the source codes, embedded images and finger prints, the database procedures and the database schemas of the pirated will contribute substantially to the reliability of cyber forensic investigation [1].

Secondly, AFC does not properly explain, how the increased-complexity of analyzing a program that is written by one programmer and updated at various instances later, by others programmers, is dealt with. As far as program logic is concerned, most programs are very likely to have the thumb impressions of many programmers due to the frequent turnover of employees in the software industry and these multiple thumb impressions, compatibly identified in both the 'original' and the 'pirated' sources, can prove to be vital in establishing piracy.

Thirdly, AFC does not offer a standard and judiciary-friendly format for presenting the result of comparison. Any judiciary system with a sense of responsibility and accountability would like to ensure that they be properly informed in matters that are outside their area of expertise [16, p.20]. This makes it incumbent on computer experts not only to provide the judicial system with such expertise but also to create general awareness for the proper utilization of such expertise. In actual terms, what the court might expect from a technical expert would be an informative report that is self-explanatory, jargon-free and non-esoteric in format. Thus, the format of expert's report becomes a matter of prime importance.

Further, it is also not clear how AFC deals with the problems of identifying programming errors and blunders in the original and of establishing their presence verbatim in the allegedly pirated. A programming error found in well-tested and implemented software can be a variable or a code segment or a field in a database table, which causes or produces wrong result during the execution of the program. A programming blunder found in well tested and implemented software can be a variable or a code segment or a field in a database table, which is hardly used or executed in the context of the application or the user's functionality but unlike an error, it will be harmless [15]. While trying to establish a variable name or a code segment as a programming blunder, the expert needs to confirm that it is (i) absent elsewhere in the original, (ii) present in the allegedly pirated exactly in the same context as it was found in the original and (iii) absent elsewhere in the allegedly pirated. Identifying programming errors and blunders in the original and establishing their presence verbatim in the allegedly pirated may additionally require expert's common sense, intuition and expertise.

One of the biggest limitations of almost all these theoretical frameworks (including AFC) is their inability to view software piracy investigation as a cyclic process. All the existing theoretical frameworks consider software piracy investigation as a linear sequential process. For instance, if an error in abstracting the software was found in the filtration stage of AFC, the need to return to the abstraction stage for necessary correction and the need for a possible modification of all the subsequent abstractions and filtrations are not clearly explained in any of these tools.

Not only the AFC test but also all the existing and established approaches and products would fail when the scope of investigation of the software piracy suit is expanded beyond comparing two software packages. While software tools, including SIMILE workshop, can yield results in software comparison, there are certain areas where only manual comparison can yield convincing result. For instance, if sundry complainant-specific data is found in the seized computer system of the alleged pirate, only manual investigation can bring this out as tangible evidence. [17]. One specific manifestation of this could be the existence of files related to the complainant's clientele or a back up copy of the live database of a client of the complainant found in the pirate's computer system. Such rare instances occur when the piracy was done by performing a disk copy (of the complainant's computer) that resulted in pirating not only the source code and data base related files but also other confidential data of the complainant [17]. The existence of such material in the seized memory is strong evidence of piracy as these are materials irrelevant for the functioning of the software and hence should not have been there at all. Another manifestation of this is a case where a UK-based software firm alleged that one of its (former) employees had appropriated a software product of his employers and was marketing it as his own even while he was still employed in the company, it was found that the alleged culprit had already created and maintained a website to market the pirated while still employed by this firm. This proof from the DNS server was enough to initiate a case in the court. None of the software piracy forensic tools has capacity to unearth such supporting evidence. This also shows that software intelligence needs to be supplemented with manual intelligence.

Where do we go from here? So, a step by step and less-complex manual procedure to compare two software packages is highly necessary for the technical experts to supplement software intelligence offered by the automated tools. Such a manual approach can be created either by further developing some existing and established procedure or by formulating a new procedure, which would cover the above mentioned limitations of abstraction and filtration. To suit the requirements of such an approach, AFC approach needs to and can be further modified.

In spite of all the advantages of AFC, there are two areas in AFC that require further explanation / modification for enhancing the effectiveness of AFC and they are abstraction and filtration. One can give clarity to the abstraction stage and thereby add value to it by further listing out various forensic investigation areas in the software namely functional area, reports generated, screens generated, menu structure, data structure, object code strings, documents, just to name a few (See also 18, pp. 317-25, and 19). Additionally, the abstraction stage also requires clear explanation as to how the abstraction process needs to be implemented in each area. The filtration stage, on the other hand, can be improved by providing an enhanced list of specific elements that are to be filtered out. The AFC list does provide a good guideline, but one needs to specifically bear in mind some of the weaknesses of the prevailing lists (for instance, absence of reference to post-piracy modifications). Above all these, the existing sequential process of AFC needs to be modified to incorporate the idea of cyclicality of the process so as to enable the expert to go back and correct errors at any previous stage and properly also attend to consequential changes in the subsequent stages in the software piracy investigation process. Finally, the addition of a totally new stage that will stress the need for presenting the results of the whole investigation in a judiciary-friendly, less-technical, jargon-less, and non-esoteric format that explain similarity, preferably in numerical terms is strongly advocated.

References

1. Santhosh Baboo, S., Vinod Bhattathiripad, P. (under editorial review): Software Piracy Forensics: Impact and Implications of post-piracy modifications. Digital Investigation - The International Journal of Digital Forensics & Incident Response (2010)
2. van der Ejik, P.: Comparative Discourse Analysis of Parallel texts, eprint arXiv:cmp-lg/9407022. Digital Equipment Corporation, Ratelaar 38, 3434 EW, Nieuwegein, The Netherlands, CMP-lg/ 9407022 (1994)
3. Yamamoto, T., Matsushita, M., Kamiya, T., Inoue, K.: Measuring Similarity of Large Software Systems Based on Source Code Correspondence. IEEE Transactions on Software Engineering, XX, Y (2004)

4. Lancaster, T., Culwin, F.: A Comparison of Source Code Plagiarism Detection Engines. Computer Science Education (2004), http://www.informaworld.com/
5. Li, C.-T.: Handbook of Research on Computational Forensics, Digital Crime, and Investigation: Methods and Solutions. In: Information Science Reference, ch. XX (2010), http://www.info-sci-ref.com
6. Frantzeskou, G., Stamatatos, E., Gritzalis, S., Chaski, C. E., Howald, B. S.: Identifying Authorship by Byte-Level N-Grams: The Source Code Author Profile (SCAP) Method. International Journal of Digital Evidence 6(1) (2007)
7. United States Court of Appeals Judge John Walker, Protectable Nuggets: Drawing the Line Between Idea and Expression in computer Program Copyright Protection, 44. Journal of the Copyright Society of USA 44(79) (1996)
8. Spafford, E.H., Weeber, S.A.: Software forensics: Can we track the code back to its authors? Purdue Technical Report CSD–TR 92–010, SERC Technical Report SERC–TR 110–P, Department of Computer Sciences, Purdue University (1992)
9. European Software Analysis Laboratory, The SIMILE Workshop: Automating the detection of counterfeit software (2007), http://www.esalab.com
10. Raysman, R., Brown, P.: Copyright Infringement of computer software and the Altai test. New York Law Journal 235(89) (2006)
11. United States District Court of Massachusetts, Memorandum and Order, Civil Action number 07-12157 PBS, Real View LLC. Vs. 20-20 Technologies, p. 2 (2010)
12. United States Court of Appeals, Second Circuit, Computer Associates International, Inc. v. Altai, Inc., 982 F.2d 693; 1992 U.S. App. LEXIS 33369; 119 A.L.R. Fed. 741; 92 Cal. Daily, Op. Service 10213, January 9, 1992, Argued, December 17, 1992, Filed (1992)
13. United States Court of Appeals, Second Circuit, Corrected Amicus Brief filed by Mark M. Arkin, Counsel of 5 computer scientists regarding software copyright and trade secret cases – Observation of Abstraction, Filtration and Comparison test, on appeal from the United States district court for the southern district of New York, on the suit Harbour Software Inc. Vs Applied Systems Inc., 97-7197L (1997)
14. Hollar, L.A.: Legal Protection Of Digital Information. BNA Books (2002)
15. Santhosh Baboo, S., Vinod Bhattathiripad, P.: Software Piracy Forensics: Exploiting Nonautomated and Judiciary-Friendly Technique'. Journal of Digital Forensic Practice 2(4), 175–182 (2009)
16. United States Court of Appeals, Second Circuit, Brief of Amici Curiae of 17 technical experts, in the case Universal City Studios, Inc., et al. Vs. Eric Corley, A/K/A Emmanuel Goldstein and 2600 enterprises (2001)
17. Vinod Bhattathiripad, P.: Judiciary-friendly computer forensics, Kerala Law Times, Part 13 & Index, June 29, p. 54 (2009)
18. Davis, R.: The nature of software and its consequences for establishing and evaluating piracy. Software Law Journal 5(2), 317–325 (1992)
19. Kremen, S.H.: Presentation of Technical Evidence by Experts in Computer Related Intellectual Property Litigation. Computer Forensics Online 2(1) (1998)

A Simple Cost-Effective Framework for iPhone Forensic Analysis

Mohammad Iftekhar Husain[1], Ibrahim Baggili[2], and Ramalingam Sridhar[1]

[1] Department of Computer Science and Engineering, University at Buffalo,
The State University of New York, Buffalo, NY 14260
[2] College of Information Technology, Zayed University, UAE
{imhusain,rsridhar}@buffalo.edu, ibrahim.baggili@zayed.ac.ae

Abstract. Apple iPhone has made significant impact on the society both as a handheld computing device and as a cellular phone. Due to the unique hardware system as well as storage structure, iPhone has already attracted the forensic community in digital investigation of the device. Currently available commercial products and methodologies for iPhone forensics are somewhat expensive, complex and often require additional hardware for analysis. Some products are not robust and often fail to extract optimal evidence without modifying the iPhone firmware which makes the analysis questionable in legal platforms. In this paper, we present a simple and inexpensive framework (iFF) for iPhone forensic analysis. Through experimental results using real device, we have shown the effectiveness of this framework in extracting digital evidence from an iPhone.

Keywords: iPhone, Forensics, Smartphone, Jailbreaking, iTunes.

1 Introduction

The Apple iPhone is among the most popular smart phones on the market, since its release in July 2007. According to a recent report on market share of mobile devices by Gartner [1], Apple's share of worldwide smart phone sales grew from 5.3 percent in the first quarter of 2008 to 10.8 percent in the first quarter of 2009. In terms of unit sales, iPhone jumped from 1.7 million in the first quarter of 2008 to 3.9 million during the same period in 2009. Though many smart phones have functionalities similar to iPhone, user interface and prevalence of numerous applications make them popular among many. The iPhone 3rd Generation Cellular Communication device, widely known as iPhone 3G was released in July, 2008 which has featured GPS service and faster Internet connection. Considering the mobility and functional similarity to standard computing devices, experts predict that iPhone can soon become a handy choice for cyber criminals. So, it is important for forensic community to focus on developing sound forensic methods for iPhone, forecasting the potential use of it in cyber crimes.

There are efforts from both commercial and individual forensic experts on iPhone forensics. Commercial products include Aceso by Radio Tactics [2], UFED from Cellebrite [3], Device Seizure by Paraben [4], .XRY by Micro Systemation [5] and

I. Baggili (Ed.): ICDF2C 2010, LNICST 53, pp. 27–37, 2011.

CellDEK by LogiCube [6]. However, these products can be expensive (up to multiple thousand dollars), requires additional hardware and functionality is limited only to the built-in features provided. Also, some approaches alter the firmware of iPhone to access the storage area using a method widely known as "jailbreaking" which is copyright infringement and illegal [7]. It also violates the Association of Chief Police Officers (ACPO) guideline for computer forensics and electronic evidence [8], which clearly states that "No action taken by law enforcement agencies or their agents should change data held on a computer or storage media which may be subsequently be relied upon in court."

In this paper, we propose a forensic framework for iPhone which simple to perform and free from the requirement of additional devices. In addition, this approach does not alter the iPhone firmware which keeps the digital evidence acceptable in legal venues. Using an iPhone device, we show the effectiveness of the framework in retrieving various digital artifacts. Additionally, we show the soundness of the evidence through comparisons to existing approaches using forensic standards. A preliminary version of this framework was tested on iPhone instant messaging forensics in [9].

2 Literature Review

The Apple iPhone OS is an optimized version of Mac OS X. There are two partitions on the iPhone storage device. The first partition is the system partition (approx. 300 MB). This partition includes the operating system and the default applications. The remaining space is partitioned as the user data (or media) partition. This space is where all music, contact, SMS as well as other user data are stored. When an iPhone is connected to a computer, it communicates with it using Apple File Communication protocol and creates a backup folder of user and device configuration data on it. Forensic acquisition of iPhone data can take different approaches such as acquiring the backup folder to analyze available data or obtain a physical image of the storage device.

Commercially available iPhone forensic products such as Aceso, UFED, Device Seizure, .XRY and CellDEK have some common drawbacks. Some products require additional hardware to perform the forensic analysis such as Aceso, UFED and Cell-DEK . Prices of most products vary from one to fifteen thousand USD according to our survey [10]. In addition, none of these solutions guarantees a complete recovery of device data.

Individual effort such as Zdziarski [11] approaches this problem through a bit-by-bit copy of the physical data in the iPhone. However, this approach modifies a read-only system partition which may eventually make the evidence questionable at legal venues. Forensic experts [12] extensively reviewed this approach and commented "I feel certain that without 15+ years of highly technical experience, I would have likely failed or would have certainly taken much longer to succeed (and perhaps sacrifice the iPhone data a few times along the way)." Efforts that use "jailbreaking" modify the user data partition of the iPhone opening it for legal challenges according to ACPO guideline.

3 Proposed Method

We propose a simple and cost-effective forensic framework for iPhone. Our framework contains all three phases of forensic data acquisition, data analysis and data reporting. Figure 1 depicts the overall structure of proposed iPhone forensic framework (iFF).

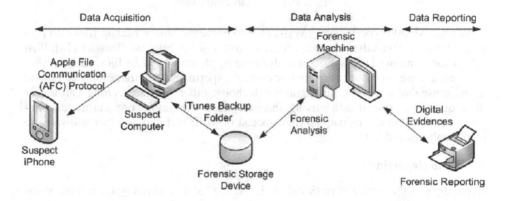

Fig. 1. Framework for iPhone Forensic Analysis

3.1 Data Acquisition

In our framework, forensic data acquisition from the suspect iPhone is based on acquiring the iPhone backup data from a machine on which the iPhone synchronized iTunes software exists. Alternatively, a forensic investigator can force backup an iPhone to a forensic examination machine using iTunes. On a Windows machine, the iTunes software saves logical copies of files on iPhone at: C:/Users/UserName/ AppData/Roaming/AppleComputer/MobileSync/Backup. By right-clicking on the device icon, when the iPhone is connected to a computer via iTunes, one can choose the backup option to backup a logical copy of iPhone data. Once the folder is acquired, the forensic investigator can use appropriate data integrity techniques and store a copy of it to a designated forensic storage device for further analysis.

3.2 Data Analysis

Depending on the iPhone firmware version, the iTunes backup folder might contain slightly different contents. In firmware version 2.0 and older, it contains mdbackup files where the actual data and the metadata reside together. The metadata describes where the actual data exists originally on the device. In some 2.0 and all 3.0 versions, the data and metadata are kept in two separate files, .mdinfo file contains only the metadata portion and .mddata contains the actual data. These binary files need to be processed to be human readable lists and databases. In our framework, we perform the data analysis as shown in Figure 2.

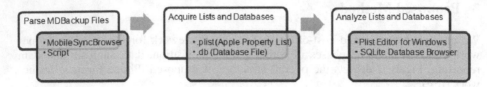

Fig. 2. Data Analysis Framework

We use MobileSyncBrowser (MSB) [13] to parse the binary backup files into lists and databases. To analyze database files, we use SQLite Database Browser [14]. Plist Editor for Windows [15] is used to analyze the Apple Property List files. Although we have used these three softwares in our current experiment, our framework is generic in the sense that a forensic investigator can choose other software as long as it serves the required purpose of data parsing and analysis. For example, one can write a simple script to parse the mdbackup files instead of MSB and choose other softwares to read databases and lists.

3.3 Data Reporting

Depending on the nature of retrieved evidence, the forensic investigator can use suitable reporting format to present it to appropriate authority. This report may be a written report, oral testimony, or some combination of the two. The investigator should adhere to RFC 4998 "Evidence Record Syntax (ERS)" [16] whenever possible.

4 Experimental Results

For this experiment, we used an iPhone third generation with firmware version 3.0 which is not jailbroken. The phone was heavily used including: Email, contacts and calendar, web browsing, phone calls, text messages, multiple Wi-Fi networks, camera images, and songs via iTunes, YouTube movies, Google maps and notes. For privacy reasons, personal information will be redacted as needed throughout the experiment.

The following is a list of digital evidence that can be found by analyzing the data from iPhone using our proposed framework.

4.1 Voice Communication Related Evidence

The backup of iPhone data contains most of call related information. For example: the *callhistory.db* (figure 3) file under Library folder contains recent call history with timestamp and duration. The *voicemail.db* file contains information regarding the received voicemails including callback number, timestamp and duration. Each voicemail is given a unique identifier. The actual content of the voicemail is saved as identifier.amr narrow band content file. A *.token* file contains credential which is used to retrieve voicemails from the cellular provider.

4.2 Text Communication Related Evidence

Three types of text communication related evidence can be recovered from the backup folder: e-mail, instant messaging (IM) and short text messaging (SMS). Information

File   Edit   View   Help

Database Structure | Browse Data | Execute SQL |

Table: | Call |

	ROWID	address	date	duration
1	3786	716	1254354538	262
2	3787	917	1254354927	181
3	3788	716	1254355247	72
4	3789	716	1254358181	10
5	3790	716	1254358242	0
6	3791	716	1254396692	0
7	3792	716	1254397074	0
8	3793	716	1254397948	0
9	3794	716	1254398014	136

Fig. 3. Voice Communication Related Evidence

on the e-mail accounts set up on built in iPhone application can be found at *com.apple.accountsettings.plist* file (figure 4). It includes the SMTP and IMAP server name, authentication type, user name and e-mail address. A significant amount of information on instant messaging can also be found. For example, Encrypted password and Yahoo! ID can be found in *com.yahoo.messenger.plist* file in preferences folder. This file also contains the time when a particular user last accessed the IM service from the iPhone. Conversations with timestamps are found in yahoo-*accountname.db* file. *yAddressBook_accountname.xml* contains the buddy list. Evidence from the conversation are found at the *session.log.db* file. Similar information can be recovered for other IM applications such as AIM. The file *sms.db* contains the entire short messages including timestamp and contents.

4.3   Network Related Evidence

Logical acquisition data from an iPhone contains both cellular and Wi-Fi network related information. For example, *com.apple.wifi.plist* file contains the name of all the networks accessed including their SSID, type of encryption, user name, date and time the network was last accessed (figure 5). Historical network TCP/IP assignments with timestamps can be found at *com.apple.network.identification.plist*. The file CSIDATA contains GSM network options and settings.

4.4   Audio-Visual Evidence

The DCIM folder contains images captured by the iPhone as .jpeg files. Each image contains the date and time when the image was originally captured as well as other image properties such as resolution, bit depth, and color scheme. Some iPhone screenshots are also saved in this folder as *.png* files. The Recordings folder contains recorded voice memos as *.m4a* (Mpeg 4 Audio) files. A separate database file *recordings.db* contains the list of all recorded files with duration time.

4.5   Location Related Evidence

Because of the default GPS capability, the iPhone backup folder contains a considerable amount of location related information. The *history.plist* file at Map folder

Fig. 4. Text Communication Related Evidence

Fig. 5. Network Related Evidence

contains the information of places searched by the iPhone user. *com.apple.maps.plist* file contains the information on last searched location and last user location with timestamp.

4.6   Online Activity Related Evidence

Online activity of the user leaves a large amount of traces in the backup data. In the Safari folder, *bookmarks.plist* contains the bookmarks saved by the user. *history.plist* contains the list of all URLs visited by the user with timestamp and visit count (figure 6). *suspendedStates.plist* saves the information of the web pages being accessed before the safari application was suspended. *com.apple.youtube.plist* contains the accessed YouTube video history (figure 7). Information regarding online games can also be found.

```
756                   <key>lastVisitedDate</key>
757                   <string>275999221.5</string>
758                   <key>redirectURLs</key>
759   ⊟               <array>
760                       <string>http://www.d-forensics.org/</string>
761                   </array>
762                   <key>title</key>
763                   <string>ICDF2C 2009</string>
764                   <key>visitCount</key>
765                   <integer>1</integer>
```

Fig. 6. Online Activity Related Evidence-1

4.7   User Activity Related Evidence

AddressBook.sqlitedb database contains two important tables. *ABPerson* contains the contacts list. *ABRecent* contains the name and e-mail addresses with timestamp to whom the user has replied or sent mails recently using iPhone's inbuilt mail applications. *Calendar.sqlitedb* database also contains some important tables. Events table contains all the registered events including location and time. It also contains alarm information. The *notes.db* file contains the contents of user notes with creation date and time. The Keyboard folder contains a default key logger file called dynamic-text.dat file. Apple iPhone uses this file to provide auto complete feature.

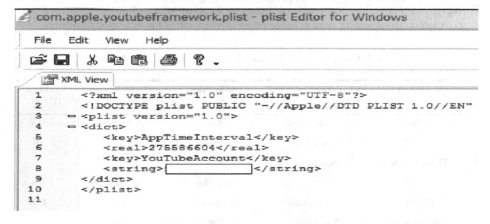

Fig. 7. Online Activity Related Evidence-2

5 Evaluations of the Digital Evidence

According to RFC 3227 "Guidelines for Evidence Collection and Archiving" [17], the legal considerations of collected evidence should be:

Admissible: Evidence must conform to certain legal rules before it can be put before a court. In our framework, we strictly follow the ACPO guidelines to make evidence sound in legal venues.

Authentic: There has to be a way to tie evidentiary materials to the incident. In the iFF framework, we recover different types of digitals evidence which make it possible to tie it to the incident according to necessity.

Complete: It must tell the whole story and not just a particular perspective. Our proposed framework retrieves a large amount of evidence to give the snapshot of the overall occurrence.

Reliable: Evidence collection method has to be free from doubts about its authenticity and veracity. As our framework follows the clearly stated procedures in Figure 1 and 2, reliability is maintained throughout the evidence collection.

Believable: It must be readily believable and understandable by a court. The digital evidence retrieved by our framework is in human readable format and it can be quickly reproduced in the courtroom for authenticity.

6 Comparisons with Existing Products and Methods

Table 1 compares our framework iFF with the existing commercial iPhone forensics products discussed in the literature review. The second column compares whether the product requires an additional hardware or standalone device. This information is taken from the product information webpage of respective companies. Next column compares, whether these products can retrieve media file (contacts, call log, sms, images etc.) related evidence. All the approaches show good performance in this feature. However, in recovering configuration files (application information, settings, and network related information), performance of Aceso and UFED is not satisfactory.

Table 1. Comparison of iFF with Existing Products and Methods

Method	Additional HW	Media Files	Configuration Files	Price (USD)
Aceso	Required	Yes	Unknown	NA
UFED	Required	Incomplete	No	4K
Device Seizure	Not Required	Yes	Yes	1K
.XRY	Not Required	Incomplete	Incomplete	9K
CellDEK	Required	Incomplete	Yes	15K
iFF (proposed)	Not Required	Yes	Yes	<50

The last column compares prices of these products found at Paraben Forensics product comparison webpage [10]. In our framework, only MobileSyncBrowser charges a very nominal fee of USD20 for parsing the backup files. Plist Editor for Windows and SQLite Database Explorer are freeware. This brings the cost of executing our forensic framework below USD50 which is quite inexpensive compared to other products. Table 2 shows the detailed comparison of extracted media files from commercial products [12] with our approach. Table 3 shows the comparison of configuration files.

Table 2. Comparison of Extracted Media Files

	Aceso	UFED	Device Seizure	.XRY	CellDEK	iFF
Call Logs	Yes	Yes	Yes	Yes	Yes	Yes
SMS	Yes	Yes	Yes	Yes	Yes	Yes
Contact	Yes	Yes	Yes	Yes	Yes	Yes
Calendar	Yes	No	Yes	Yes	Yes	Yes
Notes	Yes	No	Yes	Yes	Yes	Yes
Images	Unknown	Yes	Yes	Yes	Yes	Yes
Audio	Unknown	Yes	Yes	No	No	Yes

Table 3. Comparison of Extracted Configuration Files

	Aceso	UFED	Device Seizure	.XRY	CellDEK	iFF
Web History	Unknown	No	Yes	Yes	Yes	Yes
Bookmarks	Unknown	No	Yes	Yes	Yes	Yes
App Info	Unknown	No	Yes	Yes	Yes	Yes
Passwords	Unknown	No	Yes	No	No	Yes
Lists/XML	Unknown	No	Yes	Yes	Yes	Yes
Phone Info	Unknown	Yes	Yes	Yes	Yes	Yes
Wi-Fi Info	Unknown	No	Yes	No	Yes	Yes
HTML	Unknown	Yes	No	No	Yes	Yes

7 Challenges and Limitations

Despite the proposed method's advantages over other existing forensic methods, there are some challenges and limitations. These challenges are listed and briefly discussed below.

Most of the existing methods cannot bypass the pass-code mechanism and encryption if it is enabled. However, the proposed method inherently captures this fact and overcome this issue by taking the suspect computer into custody as one can still gain access to the iPhone even with the pass-code protection on if iPhone pairing files are captured from an iPhone backup.

Jailbreaking is a term used by iPhone users that wish to install applications that are not authorized by Apple. The jailbreaking process allows users access to the iPhone's file system. It would be critical to investigate if the proposed method is affected by jailbreaking the iPhone.

Understanding the backup structure of the iPhone may not be a onetime task. With the different generation of iPhones hitting the market, and the different firmware versions, the data structure of the backup may change. This in return pushes researchers to continuously investigate the iTunes backup structure.

We notice that with the various iPhone updates, Apple is keen on taking security measures that may impact iPhone forensics. It is critical to understand how current security updates, and future updates as well, may affect the proposed method [18] [19] [20] [21] [22].

The proposed method has the limitation of logical acquisition from the iPhone. Because, the data is logically acquired from the iPhone, all the deleted data may not be available in the backup. There are other methods, like the Zdziarski [11] method which performs a physical acquisition of the iPhone, enabling the forensic examiner to retrieve data that has been deleted. A research study confirms that the physical acquisition method was the method capable of retrieving deleted data from the iPhone [12].

8 Conclusion

In this paper, we present a simple forensic framework for iPhone. The approach is cost efficient and does not include complex tasks difficult to be performed by a forensic investigator. It follows the ACPO guideline and RFC 3227 for evidence collection and archiving to keep the recovered digital evidence sound in legal venues. Comparison of our framework with existing products also showed significant promise. We believe that our approach will be beneficial for both forensic researchers and investigators who want to experience legally sound iPhone forensics in an uncomplicated and cost effective manner.

References

1. Milanesi, C., Gupta, A., Vergne, H., Sato, A., Nguyen, T., Zimmermann, A., Cozza, R.: Garner Technology Business Research Insight. In: Dataquest Insight: Market Share for Mobile Devices, 1Q09,
    http://www.gartner.com/DisplayDocument?id=984612
2. Radio Tactics Ltd.: Aceso - Mobile forensics wrapped up. In: Radio Tactics | Mobile Phone Forensics, http://www.radio-tactics.com/products/aceso/
3. Cellebrite Forensics: Cellebrite Mobile Data Synchronization UFED Standard Kit. In: Cellebrite Mobile Data Synchronization,
    http://www.cellebrite.com/UFED-Standard-Kit.html
4. Paraben Corporation: Cell Phone Forensics. In: Paraben Corporation, Cell Phone Forensics Software, http://www.paraben-forensics.com/cell_models.html

5. Micro Systemation: XRY Physical Software. In: XRY the complete mobile forensic solution, http://www.msab.com/products/xry0/overview/page.php
6. Logicube: Logicube CellDEK Cell Phone Data Extraction. In: Logicube.com, hard drive duplication, copying hard drive & computer forensics, http://www.logicubeforensics.com/products/hd_duplication/celldek.asp
7. Lohmann, F.: Apple Says iPhone Jailbreaking is Illegal | Electronic Frontier Foundation. In: Electronice Frontier Foundation, Defending Freedom in the Digital World, http://www.eff.org/deeplinks/2009/02/apple-says-jailbreaking-illegal
8. Association of Chief Police Officers: Good Practice Guide for Computer based Electronic Evidence. In: Association of Chief Police Officers, http://www.dataclinic.co.uk/ACPO%20Guide%20v3.0.pdf (accessed June 2010)
9. Husain, M., Sridhar, R.: iForensics: Forensic Analysis of Instant Messaging on Smart Phones. In: Goel, S. (ed.) ICDF2C 2009. Lecture Notes of the Institute for Computer Sciences, Social Informatics and Telecommunications Engineering, vol. 31, pp. 9–18. Springer, Heidelberg (2010)
10. Paraben Corporation: Forensic Software Comparison Chart. In: Paraben Corporation, Cell Phone Forensics, http://www.paraben-forensics.com/cell-phone-forensics-comparison.html
11. Zdziarski, J.: iPhone Forensics. O'reilly Media, Sebastopol (2008)
12. Hoog, A., Gaffaney, K.: iPhone Forensics. In: viaForensics, http://viaforensics.com/wpinstall/wp-content/uploads/2009/03/iPhone-Forensics-2009.pdf
13. Vaughn, S.: MobileSyncBrowser | View and Recover Your iPhone Data. In: Mobile-SyncBrowser | View and Recover Your iPhone Data, http://homepage.mac.com/vaughn/msync/
14. Piacentini, M.: SQLite Database Browser. In: SQLite Database Browser, http://sqlitebrowser.sourceforge.net/
15. VOWSoft Ltd.: Plist Editor For Windows. In: Download iPod software for Windows, http://www.icopybot.com/plistset.exe
16. Gondrom, T., Brandner, R., Pordesch, U.: Electronic Record Syntex. Request For Comments 4998, Open Text Corporation (2007)
17. Brezinski, D., Killalea, T.: Guidelines for Evidence Collection and Archiving. Request For Comments 3227, In-Q-Tel (2002)
18. Apple Inc.: About the security content of the IPhone 1.1.1 Update, http://support.apple.com/kb/HT1571
19. Apple Inc.: About the security content of IPhone v1.1.3 and iPod touch v1.1.3, http://support.apple.com/kb/HT1312
20. Apple Inc.: About the security content of IPhone v2.1, http://support.apple.com/kb/HT3129
21. Apple Inc.: About the security content of IPhone OS 3.0 Software Update, http://support.apple.com/kb/HT3639
22. Apple Inc.: About the security content of IPhone OS 3.1 and IPhone OS 3.1.1 for iPod touch, http://support.apple.com/kb/HT3860
23. Apple Inc.: Apple iPhone. In: Apple-iPhone-Mobile Phone, iPod, and Internet Device, http://www.apple.com/iphone/

Detecting Intermediary Hosts by TCP Latency Measurements

Gurvinder Singh, Martin Eian, Svein Y. Willassen, and Stig Fr. Mjølsnes

Department of Telematics,
Norwegian University of Science and Technology
{gurvinde,eian,sventy,sfm}@item.ntnu.no

Abstract. Use of intermediary hosts as stepping stones to conceal tracks is common in Internet misuse. It is therefore desirable to find a method to detect whether the originating party is using an intermediary host. Such a detection technique would allow the activation of a number of countermeasures that would neutralize the effects of misuse, and make it easier to trace a perpetrator. This work explores a new approach in determining if a host communicating via TCP is the data originator or if it is acting as a mere TCP proxy. The approach is based on measuring the inter packet arrival time at the receiving end of the connection only, and correlating the observed results with the network latency between the receiver and the proxy. The results presented here indicate that determining the use of a proxy host is possible, if the network latency between the originator and proxy is larger than the network latency between the proxy and the receiver. We show that this technique has potential to be used to detect connections were data is sent through a TCP proxy, such as remote login through TCP proxies, or rejecting spam sent through a bot network.

Keywords: TCP, Latency, Intermediary Host, Proxy Server, Botnet, Intrusion Detection, Cyber Security.

1 Introduction

The use of intermediary hosts as stepping stones to conceal tracks is common in Internet misuse. By using intermediary hosts, the misuser will make it significantly more difficult to trace and detect his origins. When intermediaries are used as stepping stones, the investigator has to identify the communicating host was a stepping stone, and take steps to secure evidence on that host. This process may be cumbersome, especially if the stepping stones are located in different jurisdictions [7].

Further, there might be no evidence in the intermediary host that can be used for further tracing, either because the investigation has taken too long, or because the intermediary host has been specifically configured to avoid recording anything about the originator. Previous research has identified stepping stones to be particularly common during computer intrusions. In these instances, remote

I. Baggili (Ed.): ICDF2C 2010, LNICST 53, pp. 38–54, 2011.

attackers have been found to log in by remote shell through several intermediaries, effectively using them as TCP proxies [2].

Recent research has also revealed that spread of spam by the use of intermediary hosts is common. These intermediaries have been found to be computers infected by malicious programs and are used as SOCKS proxies without the owners' knowledge or consent [13]. It is desirable to find a method to detect if the communicating party is using an intermediary. This would allow activation of a number of countermeasures that would neutralize the effects of the misuse, and make it easier to trace the perpetrator. It would for example be possible for a mail server to stop receiving email messages from such SMTP requests or login server to deny entry for connections via an intermediary, or perhaps to activate more verbose logging and notify a system administrator.

In this work, we propose a novel approach for detecting whether the host initiating a TCP connection is an intermediary or not. The approach is based on the observation that data in certain situations arrive in bursts, and the interval between the bursts depends on the network latency of the different steps between the receiver and the originator of the data. If the network latency between the client and the proxy is larger than the observed latency between the proxy and the server, it can be inferred that the traffic is passing through one or more intermediaries.

Several researchers have studied the problem of detecting stepping stones in the past. Staniford-Chen and Heberlein proposed using traffic content thumb prints to find correlation between traffic on both sides of an intermediary [15]. This approach has been extended by several authors to also allow detection for encrypted traffic by recognizing the timing information on the connection [11,5,12]. Others have studied the limitations of these approaches under active countermeasures [18]. Coskun and Memon propose steppingstone detection based on the timing and correlation of ingress-egress packet flows at the network border [4].

These approaches all require measurement points in the network distributed in such a way that there is at least one measurement point on each side of the intermediary. In this work, no measurement point in the network path is assumed. Instead, we investigate the possibility to infer the existence of a TCP proxy from observations at the receiving host end alone.

The experiments in this work have been conducted in a controlled lab environment where the delay conditions in the lab shows similar behavior as for the Internet environment. We focus here on investigating the feasibility and the potential for this new technique of detecting intermediary hosts, which we answer positively. The next step will be to consider the network congestion, effects of application layer protocols, and other effects of observed network behavior.

2   Background

Transmission Control Protocol (TCP) is the prevalent transmission protocol on the Internet. TCP implements mechanisms to control the data rate to the network conditions, including bandwidth, latency of the connection and speed of the receiving host. Network latency between two hosts on a network can be defined as the amount of time elapsed from data has been sent from the sending host until it has been received at the destination host. On the Internet, network latency between two communicating hosts is the sum of the latencies in all the routers and network links between the communicating hosts. Network latency between two hosts on the Internet can be measured by sending icmp echo request packets from one of the hosts to the other. Unless configured to do otherwise, the other host will then reply with icmp echo reply packets, and the time elapsed between sending echo request and receiving the reply is equal to the round trip time (Δ) of the connection.

$$\Delta = 2 * (\delta_{prop} + \delta_{proc} + \delta_{queue}) \tag{1}$$

where δ_{prop} is the propagation delay, δ_{proc} is the delay caused by routers and end hosts while processing the packets and δ_{queue} is the delay caused by waiting time in the router and end hosts's queue.

The network latency can be approximated as half the value of round trip time. This measurement can be done with the ping command. However, some network service provider have special QoS class for echo packets to show the better service. In the paper, we used the value of Δ computed during the TCP 3-way handshake to avoid the special QoS class case for the ping packets.

The TCP control mechanisms include various algorithms designed to transmit the data from the sender to the receiver as efficiently as possible, while adjusting to the current conditions of the network and avoiding overloading the network. One of these mechanisms is the TCP flow control [1] and another is the Nagle [10] Algorithm. These algorithms are of special interest, since their application result in a possibility to observe network latency in a TCP data flow. In flow control mechanism, TCP window size limits the amount of unacked data in to the network and results in a possibility to observe the network latency.

TCP uses the Nagle Algorithm to adjust the sending rate of traffic where small amounts of data arrive at the TCP-layer frequently. The Nagle Algorithm works by inhibiting the sender from sending new TCP segments if any previously transmitted data on a connection remains unacknowledged [10]. New TCP data can be sent immediately only in two cases: First, if the TCP connection is just established or it was idle for some time. Second, if the size of the data to be sent is larger than the Maximum Segment Size (MSS) and the available window size of the receiver is also larger than MSS. If none of these conditions are satisfied, TCP will wait until an ACK has been received for the previously transmitted data until data is transmitted. As a result, data will be sent in bursts with intervals in between. The length of the interval is equal to the time it takes for the ack for the previously sent data to arrive. In other words, the burst interval depends on the value of Δ in the connection between the two hosts.

3 Latency Propagation Theory

The underlying observation motivating this research is that the TCP flow control causes network traffic to be sent in bursts where the interval between each burst

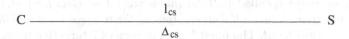

C ——————————————————————————— S
l_{cs}
Δ_{cs}

Fig. 1. A TCP connection between client C and server S on link l_{cs} with Δ_{cs} round trip time

depends on the network latency. This property holds for example in the case of a large file transfer, whereas in typical remote login protocols this property only holds if the Nagle algorithm is in use.

The idea is that if these bursts are detectable when data traffic is sent via a TCP-level *proxy*, then analysis of bursts and their intervals can be used at the receiving end to determine if the observed sender is the original sender or a TCP proxy.

Consider a connection as shown in Fig 1 on a link l_{cs} between a client C and a server S having round trip time value equal to Δ_{cs}. On the link l_{cs}, the TCP traffic can be either interactive type with small size segments or traffic due to a large file transfer with large size segments. When the transmitted data is *interactive traffic*, such as remote login and remote desktop session, then the Nagle Algorithm is applied to the traffic. Exceeding the Maximum Segment Size will enable the Nagle Algorithm.

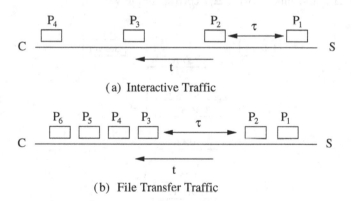

(a) Interactive Traffic

(b) File Transfer Traffic

Fig. 2. Behavior of TCP burst interarrival time (τ) with (a) interactive and (b) file transfer traffic type

With a TCP connection between client C and server S with round trip time Δ_{cs}, an observer at the server S can now observe the traffic pattern of the incoming data from the client C. The behavior observed by the observer will look similar to the pattern as shown in *part (a)* of Fig 2. Since the sender C will have to wait for unacked data to be acked before it can send more data, there will be an interval τ of value at least equal to Δ_{cs} between the data bursts from C as observed from S, as shown in Fig 2.

The time interval τ is called as *Burst Interarrival Time(BIT)*, which is defined as the *time difference between the arrival time of the received burst and the arrival time of the previous burst*. The burst length in case of interactive traffic is equal to single packet, due to the small data size.

Now assume the received traffic at server S is of type file transfer and thus the segment size is large. Now the Nagle algorithm will not be involved in limiting the client C, however the TCP flow control mechanism limits the client C by *CWND* window size in sending large numbers of segments. In the initial phase of the connection, the window size is equal to 2-3 segments. Subsequently, the client C waits for an ack to arrive from server S. This will result in a time interval τ which will be of value comparable to Δ_{cs}. This pattern is shown in the *pat b)* of Fig 2. The value of delay between packet P_1 and P_2 is very small as both segments are sent together by client C. But after sending 2 segments client C waits for an ack to arrive and therefore the next burst of packets will arrive after interval τ of value comparable to Δ_{cs}.

$$ C \underset{\Delta_{cp}}{\overset{l_{cp}}{\rule{0pt}{0pt}\hspace{4cm}}} P \underset{\Delta_{ps}}{\overset{l_{ps}}{\rule{0pt}{0pt}\hspace{4cm}}} S $$

Fig. 3. TCP connections between client C and proxy P, and proxy P and server S on link l_{cp} with Δ_{cp} and link l_{ps} with Δ_{ps} correspondingly

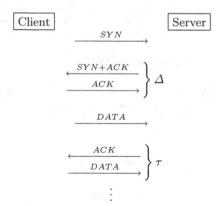

Fig. 4. The TCP threeway handshake and data segments measurements of the round trip time Δ, and the burst interarrival time τ

Now consider the connection setup of Fig 3, where P is acting as a TCP proxy. In this case, an observer at server S may not know that P is acting as a proxy, and may erroneously believe that the host P is the originator of the communication.

Data received at P from C is immediately forwarded to S by the proxy program running at P. Thus, when segments arrive at P, the data will already be in bursts, with burst interval depending on Δ_{cp}. The resulting interval between data bursts perceived by the observer at S will then depend on both Δ_{cp} and Δ_{ps}.

We hypothesize that the burst interval observed at the server S will depend on the largest of Δ_{cp} or Δ_{ps}. If Δ_{cp} is larger than Δ_{ps}, the burst interval as observed at S will depend on Δ_{cp} and not on Δ_{ps}. If this is the case, an observer at S can use the burst interval to determine if P is the real originator of the connection, by measuring the Δ_{ps} and comparing with the observed burst intervals τ. See Fig. 4.

4   Statistical Model of Burst Inter-arrival Time

The purpose of our statistical model is to distinguish between the l_{cs} connection and the l_{ps} connection. We construct a model of the l_{cs} connection to achieve this purpose. As explained in Section 3, we expect Δ_{cs} and τ to have similar values. Thus, we assume that there is a linear relationship between Δ and τ. We model the round trip time as $\Delta + \epsilon_\Delta$ and the burst inter-arrival time as $\tau + \epsilon_\tau$, where ϵ_Δ and ϵ_τ represent the random errors in δ_{prop}, δ_{proc} and δ_{queue}.

We have to make several assumptions to be able to construct a hypothesis test. We assume that ϵ_Δ and ϵ_τ are independent and identically distributed. This assumption implies that the network is not congested, and that none of the nodes have strained computational or memory resources. Furthermore, we assume that ϵ_Δ and ϵ_τ follow a normal distribution. The normality assumption is investigated empirically in Section 5.

We use simple linear regression with Δ as the independent variable and τ as the dependent variable to model the linear relationship between Δ and τ . The slope b and intersection a can be estimated based on an experiment with n samples, where each of the samples is a tuple (Δ_i, τ_i). The simple linear regression model is based on the assumption that the independent variable is exact, which is not the case in our experiments. However, the model still provides an unbiased estimate of the slope b and intersection a of the linear relationship. We also used an orthogonal regression model to verify that the results of the simple linear regression were unbiased. The orthogonal regression model resulted in the same parameters a and b.

We use the linear regression model to construct a prediction interval for the τ values to be observed. (Walpole et al. [17, p.410] or other basic statistics textbook will explain how to construct a prediction interval for a simple linear regression model.) Under the assumptions presented above, a $100(1 - \alpha)\%$ one-sided prediction interval is:

$$\{(\Delta_0, \tau_0) | \tau_0 < a + b\Delta_0 + t_\alpha s \sqrt{1 + \frac{1}{n} + \frac{(\Delta_0 - \overline{\Delta})^2}{\sum_{i=1}^{n}(\Delta_i - \overline{\Delta})^2}}\} \qquad (2)$$

where

$$s = \sqrt{\frac{\sum_{i=1}^{n}(\tau_i - \overline{\tau})^2 - b\sum_{i=1}^{n}(\Delta_i - \overline{\Delta})(\tau_i - \overline{\tau})}{n - 2}}$$

t_α is a value of the Student-T distribution with $n - 2$ degrees of freedom. $\overline{\Delta}$ represents the mean of the Δ_i values, and $\overline{\tau}$ represents the mean of the τ_i values from the linear regression.

The following hypotheses are defined to use the model for hypothesis testing:

$$H_0 : \Delta_0 = \tau_0$$

$$H_1 : \Delta_0 < \tau_0$$

H_0 represents the l_{cs} connection and H_1 represents the l_{ps} connection. A tuple (Δ_0, τ_0) can then be measured for a single connection. If the measured τ_0 value falls outside the prediction interval, H_0 is rejected and we assume that a proxy is being used.

5   Experimental Setup

Three experiments are performed to test the proposed hypothesis. The first experiment is a RTT experiment, which tests the latency behavior of the lab setup against the real world Internet latency behavior. This will show how much the setup resembles with real world and applicability of the results. The second experiment is conducted using the connection setup as shown in Fig 1. The purpose of this experiment is to see the variation in τ values under different Δ values. We made our model based on setup shown in Fig 1. The last experiment is conducted to test validity of the model to detect intermediary host under the presence of a proxy host in the connection. The setup for third experiment is shown in Fig 3. The result from all these experimets are described in section 6.

The experiments are done under controlled laboratory conditions to eliminate unknown factors and to ensure repeatability. Three computers are configured with Linux distribution Ubuntu 9.10 running kernel 2.6.31-5. These are attached to the same 100 Mb Ethernet LAN and given roles as server (S), client (C) and proxy (P). The round trip time between any of the three computers on the LAN is approximately 1 ms.

In the experimental setup data is generated at the client side and sent to the server with varying latency on the connection in between as shown in Fig 2. The arriving data bursts can then be observed at the receiving server S and the results can be checked for consistency with the hypothesis. If the results from this experiment do not refute the hypothesis, the experiment can proceed with introducing a proxy P between the client and the server as shown in Fig 3.

To generate the traffic, a different traffic generating program named Traffic Generator (TG), tool developed at SRI International and University of Southern California [9] is used. In the experiments, TG is used to generate TCP traffic on the client C and to sink the traffic at the server S. The experiments are conducted with different packet length and time distributions as described in the next section.

GNU Netcat was used as proxy [6]. Netcat is a simple utility, which reads and writes data across the network connections using TCP and UDP transport protocols. In the experiments, netcat was setup as a proxy in the following way:

```
$ mknod backpipe p
$ nc -l -v -p 1234 0<backpipe | nc 129.241.209.XXX
  1234 1>backpipe
```

When the client connects to this port and sends data to it, a new TCP connection is opened to the server (129.241.209.XXX) at port 1234 and received data is forwarded to it. Any data received in the opposite direction is forwarded back to the client through the pipe.

To observe the results on the server S, the packet sniffer Deamonlogger [14] was used. It was necessary to increase the amount of memory used for the capturing engine to avoid packets being dropped. Further, the Wireshark packet analyzer [3] was used to analyze the captured packets.

To create network latencies resembling Internet latencies in the laboratory, Netem coupled with the Traffic Control (tc) tool was used. Netem and the traffic control tool are parts of the *iproute2* package of the Linux kernel. The traffic control tool uses Netem to emulate Internet behavior. The queuing architecture of Linux kernel is shown in Figure 5. The queuing discipline sits between the protocol output and the network device. The queuing discipline is an object with two interfaces. One interface receives packet from IP protocol and another interface forwards these packets to the network device. The queuing discipline makes the decision of forwarding packet based upon the defined policies.

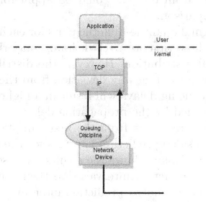

Fig. 5. Linux Queuing Architecture

6 Burst Interarrival Time Results

6.1 RTT Experiment Results

To make sure that the lab setup resembles with the real world behavior, the behavior of induced delay via netem is tested against the real world round trip delay results. An experiment has been performed to ping the Univ. of Tromsø web server from the lab system. Thus results obtained from pinging the web server are compared with the result from pinging the lab server from the same system with similar Δ values.

Four experiments are performed to compare our lab setup to a real world scenario and to investigate how close the Δ values follow a normal distribution. Two experiments are performed on the lab setup, and two experiments are performed on the Internet connection. The Internet connection from the lab to the University of Tromsø has no preferential treatment of ICMP packets. 100,000 ICMP echo requests are issued in each experiment, and the Δ value recorded with microsecond accuracy.

Table 1. Results from the RTT validation experiment

Scenario	# Samples	Median	Mean	Stdev
Lab 1	100,000	$14719\mu s$	$14768\mu s$	$111\mu s$
Lab 2	99,998	$14714\mu s$	$14766\mu s$	$173\mu s$
UiT 1	99,995	$14869\mu s$	$14872\mu s$	$61\mu s$
UiT 2	100,000	$14869\mu s$	$14872\mu s$	$69\mu s$

Table 1 shows the estimated parameters of the sampling distributions for each experiment under the normality assumption. The estimated parameters show that the measurements from the real world scenario have less variance and a median closer to the mean than the measurements from our lab setup. This indicates that the results from our lab could be applicable to the real world scenario we use as a comparison.

Figure 6 shows the normal quantile-quantile plots for each of the experiments. The normal Q-Q plots show that an overwhelming majority of the measured Δ values follow a normal distribution. However, the distributions have a long right tail. This result is expected, as any deviation from the distribution due to excessive processing or queueing delays will result in a higher Δ. The lower part of the distribution is bounded by the propagation delay.

We use the estimated parameters from the first sample in each scenario to compute $100(1 - \alpha)\%$ two-sided prediction intervals for the distributions, under the normality assumption. Table 2 shows the results. We use the Student-T distribution to compute the prediction intervals. We then use the second sample in each scenario to test the estimated prediction interval. Lost packets are considered to have a Δ value higher than the prediction interval. The goals of this test are to determine how closely the prediction interval of a normal distribution matches the measured Δ values, to quantify the impact of the long right tail, and to compare the results from our lab setup to the real world scenario.

The effect of the long right tail can clearly be seen for $\alpha/2 \leq 0.001$. For these α values, none of the measured Δ values are lower than the prediction interval, but approximately 200 of the Δ values exceed the prediction interval. These are the values on the long right tail. The right tail thus puts a lower bound on the α value, where decreasing it further has little effect. The optimal value

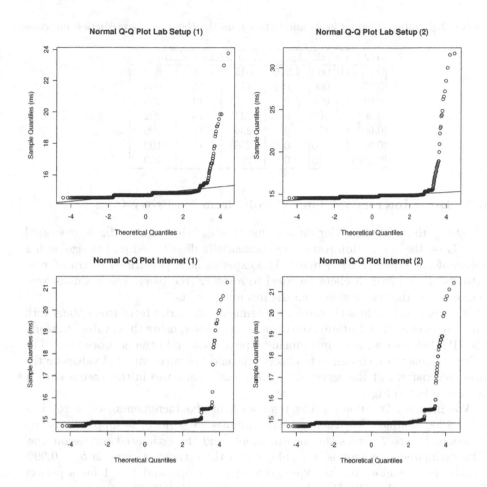

Fig. 6. Normal Q-Q plots for the RTT validation experiment. Most of the measurements follow the normal distribution, but there is a long tail to the right in each of the plots.

is $\alpha = 0.001$, where we only have to consider the one-sided prediction interval larger than the estimated mean. α represents the probability of a type I error (false positive). The lowest practical α value we are able to achieve, given the distribution of Δ, is between 0.002 and 0.003. For the rest of this paper, we will use the conservative assumption that $\alpha = 0.001$ gives a 0.5% probability of type I errors.

Finally, Table 2 also shows that for $\alpha \leq 0.001$, the results from our lab setup and the real world scenario are very similar. In both cases, a prediction interval computed under a normality assumption gives less than a 0.5% probability of type I errors for $\alpha = 0.001$. The results in Section 6 are thus applicable to the real world scenario as well.

Table 2. Number of values lower and higher than the $100(1-\alpha)\%$ prediction intervals

$\alpha/2$	$E(\Delta)$	$\Delta_{Lab} <$	$\Delta_{Lab} >$	$\Delta_{UiT} <$	$\Delta_{UiT} >$
0.1	10,000	4,216	615	51	885
0.05	5,000	4,181	443	51	606
0.01	1,000	0	237	49	299
0.005	500	0	237	49	202
0.001	100	0	236	0	199
0.0005	50	0	236	0	199
0.0001	10	0	222	0	199

6.2 Burst Interarrival Time Results from No Proxy Case

To study the TCP behavior on a connection l_{cs}, the data traffic is generated by TG on the connection using an exponentially distributed packet size with a mean of size equal to MSS bytes. The experiment is performed to transfer 10 Kbytes of data from a client (sender) to a server (receiver). The τ values were measured at the server side from the incoming bursts.

The delay (Δ) values chosen for experiments are varies from 1ms - 50ms with an increment of 1ms. Initially, the tests are conducted using these values to study the IPT behavior without introducing a proxy system in the network path. The values of delays are chosen so to observe the effect of variation of Δ values on the observed pattern at the server side. The connection setup in this case is similar to shown in the Fig 1.

We measure 20 tuples (Δ_i, τ_i) for each of the increments, for a total of $n = 1000$ samples. We then use the samples to perform a simple linear regression. Figure 7 shows the measurements and the estimated regression line. The estimated intercept is $a = 144\mu s$ and the estimated slope is $b = 0.999$, which are very close to the expected values $a = 0\mu s$ and $b = 1$ for a perfect linear relationship. The R^2 value for the regression is 0.9998.

Figure 8 shows a normal Q-Q plot of the residuals. Most of the residuals follow a normal distribution, but as in the previous experiment, the distribution has a long tail. However, the long tail starts earlier in the residuals than in the RTT experiment. Thus, the expected number of observations outside the prediction interval will be higher than in the RTT experiment. We use Formula 2 to compute a 99.9% one-sided prediction interval ($\alpha = 0.001$), which is shown in Figure 7 together with the regression line and measurements. 12 of the samples (1.2%) in the linear regression model are outside the prediction interval, so we cannot make the same conclusion as in the RTT experiment. Based on the results, a conservative assumption is that 95% of τ values to be observed fall within the 99.9% prediction interval. Thus, when we use $\alpha = 0.001$, the actual false positive rate is 5%, rather than 0.1%. The residual standard error is $179\mu s$, which is similar to the results from the previous experiments.

From the result, we have seen that the bursts arrived at the server side after corresponding delay Δ_{cs} of the l_{cs} connection. The similar behavior is seen in all the test cases. The observed behavior can be explained by the TCP flow control

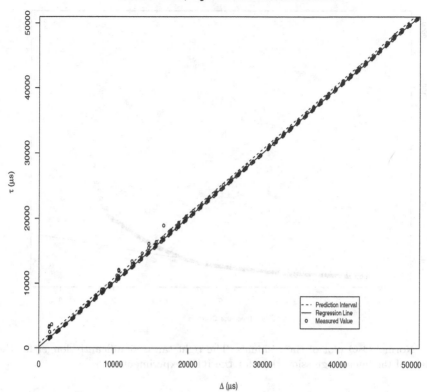

Fig. 7. The measured values, regression line and prediction interval with $\alpha = 0.001$. The number of samples outside the prediction interval is 12 (1.2% of the samples).

algorithm, which limits the amount of data to the sender by window size. The client must then wait for ACK to arrive before sending more data.

The client sends the data bursts to the server and upon receiving the data, the server acknowledges it and this acknowledgement arrives at the client side after completing journey from server to the client. This result in arrival of ACK at the client side after one complete RTT delay of the connection and the next data packet at the server end arrives after this delay. The observed data is thus consistent with the hypothesis that burst interarrival time is related to the network delay.

6.3 Burst Interarrival Time Results from Proxy Case

Now to study the TCP behavior under the presence of the proxy system, we introduce a proxy system between the server and the client. The connection setup of this test case is shown in Fig 3. The delay between server and the proxy system is set to 20ms and delay between the proxy and the client system

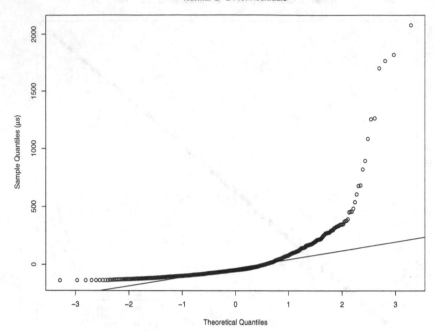

Fig. 8. Normal Q-Q plot of the residuals. The right tail is significantly longer for the residuals of the linear regression than for the RTT experiments.

is varying from 10 ms, 20 ms, 25ms, 30ms and 50ms respectively. The reason behind choosing the specific delay conditions is as, the given settings address the case when the delay on client-proxy connection is less, equal and higher than server-proxy connection. Therefore we will see the IPT behavior in all five cases.

We measure 100 samples (Δ_i, τ_i) for each of the cases $\Delta_{cp} \in \{10ms, 20ms, 25ms, 30ms, 50ms\}$. Figure 9 shows the results. The approximate prediction interval shown in the figure is based on the maximum Δ value measured to be able to illustrate the results in a single figure. We then use the linear regression model to perform the hypothesis test from Section 4 on each sample. For the cases $\Delta_{cp} \leq 20ms$, we do not detect the proxy in any of the samples. However, for the cases $\Delta_{cp} \geq 25ms$, we detect the proxy in all of the samples.

When Δ_{cp} is either 10ms or 20ms, the measured τ is approximately 20ms at the server side, which is the value of Δ_{ps}. In the other test cases, when Δ_{cp} is higher than 20ms, the measured τ at the server side is significantly higher than 20 ms. This is caused by the TCP flow control algorithm, which limits the amount of data to the sender by the window size of the connection. The client must then wait for an ACK to arrive before sending more data. Thus, in this case, the observed τ values at the server is different from what would be expected with the Δ_{ps} between the proxy and the server.

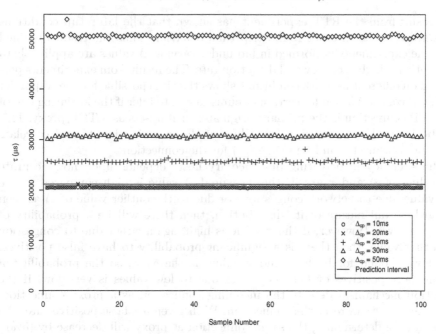

Fig. 9. An illustration of the results for the proxy case. The approximate regression line was based on the maximum Δ value measured. For the experiments where $\Delta_{cp} \leq 20ms$, we are not able to detect the proxy at all. However, for the experiments where $\Delta_{cp} \geq 25ms$, we achieve a 100% detection rate.

We observe that if Δ_{ps} is less than Δ_{cp} then it is possible to infer the presence of a proxy system from the observed τ values of the incoming bursts. The proxy system will receive data from the client within the Δ_{cp} delay of its connection with the client. As a result, the data arrive at the server side with τ values comparable to Δ_{cp}, which are higher than Δ_{ps} and make the detection of proxy system possible. The higher Δ_{cp} is relative to Δ_{ps} the higher the accuracy becomes in the detection of proxy system.

From the above results, we see that the TCP flow control algorithm behaves differently under different delay conditions. Similar behavior has been shown when the traffic with small segment size was generated and the τ values from the initial stage were compared with the Δ value of the underlying connection. This behavior was, as hypothesized, due to the Nagle algorithm, which inhibits sender from sending small size of data, until the arrival of ack of unacked data.

Thus, by monitoring the τ values of incoming bursts at the receiver end, it is possible to detect the presence of intermediary hosts by comparing the τ values against the incoming connection Δ value. If the τ value is comparable to the Δ delay of the incoming connection, then connection is most likely to be the direct connection, otherwise the connection can be marked as an incoming connection through intermediary hosts.

7 Discussion and Future Work

The result from the RTT experiment has shown that the lab setup conditions are similar to the Internet round trip time behavior. Thus the result obtained from the experiments performed in lab under varying Δ values are applicable to internet with high accuracy and detection rate. The result from experiments performed on different network conditions shows that it is possible for the responder of a TCP connection, under certain circumstances, to infer if the initiating end of the TCP connection is the primary originator or if it acts as a TCP proxy. This can be inferred by measuring (τ) values of the incoming bursts and correlate with the measured round trip time (Δ) for the connection.

The accuracy in detecting intermediary hosts depends upon how accurate the values of Δ and τ are. If the measured Δ value is high compared to the real value, due to network congestions or due to the outlier value of Δ as seen in the long tail nature of its distribution, then there will be a probability of false negatives. However, if the τ value is high, again either due to congestion or outlier value, then there is a significant probability to have false positives. The lower bound for both Δ and τ values is the δ_{prop}, so the probability of having false positives or false negatives due to low values is very low. If the detection mechanism detects the incoming connection as a proxy connection, then the server can reset the connection. With given 5% false positive rate, the probablity of determining the same connection as proxy will decrease by $(5\%)^n$ due to independence between the incoming connection, thus the probability of detecting the legitimate connection as a proxy connection vanishes exponentially. Moreover, the higher the value of Δ_{cp} is compared to Δ_{ps}, the higher the accuracy is in detection of intermediary host.

We have observed during this work that the proxy type used in the communication session influence different behaviors at the receiver end. In the above experiments, we used Netcat as a proxy, which sends the ack to the client C of received data and then forwards the data to the sever S. However, we found some programs work as a TCP level proxy, such as *iprelay* [16], which does not send the ack to the client C until they have received the ack from the server S. This behavior will result in higher τ value, which is equal to sum of the Δ values on both the connections.

The experiments in this work have been conducted in a controlled lab environment and the delay conditions in the lab have shown behavior similar to the real Internet environment. Effects of network congestion and effects of application layer protocols on the observed behavior for intermediary hosts detection are questions for further study. The generalized question related to a sequence of intermediary host connections are open for further investigated.

8 Conclusion

This work has explored the possibility of determining whether a host communicating via a TCP connection is the data originator or just acting as a TCP proxy, by the measurements of the inter packet arrival at the receiving end of the connection. Our results indicate that this is possible, if the network latency between the originator and proxy is larger than the network latency between the proxy and the responder. This novel method has applications in various domains such as rejecting malicious remote logins through TCP proxies, or reject spam messages sent through a proxy bot network, or block the access to restricted media contents when request arrives from a proxy host or detection of the Tor [8] usage in an incoming connection.

References

1. Allman, M., Paxson, V., Stevens, W.: TCP congestion control. RFC 2581 (1999)
2. Barford, P., Ullrich, J., Yegneswaran, V.: Internet intrusions: global characteristics and prevalence. In: Proceedings of the 2003 ACM SIGMETRICS Conference, pp. 138–147 (2003)
3. Combs, G.: Wireshark - packet analyzer, http://www.wireshark.org/ (accessed April 2010)
4. Coskun, B., Memon, N.: Online Sketching of Network Flows for Real-Time Stepping-Stone Detection. In: Proceedings of the 2009 Annual Computer Security Applications Conference, pp. 473–483. IEEE Computer Society, Los Alamitos (2009)
5. Etoh, H., Yoda, K.: Finding a connection chain for tracing intruders. In: Proceedings of the 6th European Symposium on Research in Computer Security, pp. 191–205. Springer, Heidelberg (2000)
6. Giacobbi, G.: The GNU netcat project, http://netcat.sourceforge.net/ (accessed April 2010)
7. Lee, S., Shields, C.: Tracing the source of network attack: A technical, legal and societal problem. In: Proceedings of the 2001 IEEE Workshop on Information Assurance and Security, pp. 239–246 (2001)
8. Mathewson, N., Dingledine, R., Syverson, P.: Tor: The second generation onion router. In: Proceedings of the 13th USENIX Security Symposium, pp. 303–320 (2004)
9. McKenney, P., Lee, D., Denny, B.: Traffic generator tool, http://www.postel.org/tg/ (accessed April 2010)
10. Nagle, J.: Congestion control in IP/TCP internetworks. RFC 896 (January 1984)
11. Paxson, V., Zhang, Y.: Detecting stepping stones. In: Proceedings of the 9th USENIX Security Symposium, pp. 171–184 (2000)
12. Reeves, D., Wang, X.: Robust correlation of encrypted attack traffic through stepping stones by manipulation of interpacket delays. In: Proceedings of the 10th ACM Conference on Computer and Communication Security, pp. 20–29 (2003)
13. Riden, J.: Know your enemy lite: Proxy threats - socks v666. Honeynet Project (August 2008), http://www.honeynet.org/papers/proxy
14. Roesch, M.: Daemonlogger, packet logger, http://www.snort.org/users/roesch/Site/Daemonlogger/Daemonlogger.htm (accessed April 2010)
15. Staniford-Chen, S., Heberlein, L.T.: Holding intruders accountable on the internet. In: SP 1995: Proceedings of the 1995 IEEE Symposium on Security and Privacy, Washington, DC, USA, p. 39. IEEE Computer Society, Los Alamitos (1995)

16. Stewart, G.: iprelay - a user-space bandwidth shaping TCP proxy daemon, http://manpages.ubuntu.com/manpages/hardy/man1/iprelay.1.html (accessed April 2010)
17. Walpole, R., Myers, R., Myers, S., Yee, K.: Probability and statistics for engineers and scientists. Macmillan, New York (2007)
18. Zhang, L., Persaud, A., Guan, Y., Johnson, A.: Stepping stone attack attribution in non-cooperative IP networks. In: Proc. of the 25th IEEE International Performance Computing and Communication Conference (IPCCC 2006), Washington, DC, USA. IEEE Computer Society, Los Alamitos (April 2006)

Reliable Acquisition of RAM Dumps from Intel-Based Apple Mac Computers over FireWire

Pavel Gladyshev[1] and Afrah Almansoori[2]

[1] Center for Cybercrime Investigation, University College Dublin
Belfield, Dublin 4, Ireland
Pavel.Gladyshev@ucd.ie
[2] Electronic Forensics Department, Dubai Police Head Quarters,
Dubai, United Arab Emirates
Almansoori@CyberCrimeTech.com

Abstract. RAM content acquisition is an important step in live forensic analysis of computer systems. FireWire offers an attractive way to acquire RAM content of Apple Mac computers equipped with a FireWire connection. However, the existing techniques for doing so require substantial knowledge of the target computer configuration and cannot be used reliably on a previously unknown computer in a crime scene. This paper proposes a novel method for acquiring RAM content of Apple Mac computers over FireWire, which automatically discovers necessary information about the target computer and can be used in the crime scene setting. As an application of the developed method, the techniques for recovery of AOL Instant Messenger (AIM) conversation fragments from RAM dumps are also discussed in this paper.

Keywords: RAM Analysis, Mac OS X, FireWire, AOL Instant Messenger (AIM).

1 Introduction

Forensic acquisition of data from a running computer system is commonly referred to as live forensics or computer forensics field triage. It is performed in situations when the extraction of evidential data through post mortem forensic analysis is either impossible or infeasible. One such situation is when the evidential data resides only in the RAM of the target computer, and would be lost if the computer was switched off.

Within this paper, the contributions to the field of live forensics are two-fold. Section 2 presents a FireWire based technique for reliably acquiring the contents of RAM whilst avoiding memory mapped input-output registers. This technique is applicable to Intel based Apple Mac computers running Mac OS X, and requires no prior knowledge of RAM size or the target system's memory map. Section 3 presents an application of this RAM imaging technique, to the task of AOL Instant Messenger (AIM) conversation fragment recovery from RAM; the process, methodology, and Perl scripts are explained in detail.

I. Baggili (Ed.): ICDF2C 2010, LNICST 53, pp. 55–64, 2011.

2 Reliable Acquisition of Mac OS X RAM Content via FireWire

2.1 State of the Arts

IEEE 1394 is a serial bus interface standard for high-speed data communication. Apple Computer Inc. uses brand name of FireWire for IEEE 1394 technology. One of the features of FireWire is that devices connected to the FireWire bus have access to each other's RAM. Several authors including M. Dornsief, et al [10], and A. Boileau [1,2] demonstrated the possibility of acquiring RAM content of the target computer over FireWire. To do so, the target computer is connected to the investigator's computer via FireWire. A special application is then executed on the investigator's computer to extract the data from the target computer's RAM. This paper refers to the acquisition of RAM content of the target computer as "RAM imaging".

The main problem with the existing approaches to FireWire RAM imaging is caused by the presence of memory mapped input-output device registers (or simply memory mapped I/O registers) in the memory address space of the target computer. Accidental reading of these registers over FireWire may trigger undesired activity in the corresponding devices and may cause instability and system crash in the target computer. The existing applications for FireWire RAM imaging, such as 1394memimage [2], need to be explicitly told which memory areas to image. To do so, the investigator needs to know the size of RAM in the target computer and the location of the memory mapped I/O register areas *apriori*. Although it is possible in incident response situations, where the investigator has the complete knowledge of the target system, it is not practical in live forensics situations, when a previously unknown live computer is found at the crime scene.

To avoid instability of the target system during FireWire RAM imaging at the crime scene, it is essential for the RAM imaging application to be able to automatically discover the location of the memory mapped I/O registers in the target computer. This research was able to develop a suitable process for Intel-based Apple Mac computers running Mac OS X operating system; this process is explained below.

2.2 Reliable FireWire RAM Imaging for Intel-Based Apple Mac Computers

The analysis of Mac OS X source code has shown that the information about the location of memory mapped I/O registers is stored in a special data structure, Memory-Map, of Mac OS X kernel. To access this data structure over FireWire, the RAM imaging application needs to identify

1. the version of Mac OS X on the target computer, and
2. the address of the MemoryMap data structure.

The following describes in detail the process and pitfalls in answering these questions.

Accessing Kernel Data Structures over FireWire. Our experiments have shown an investigator's computer connected to an Intel-based Apple Mac via FireWire can access the first 4GiB of the Apple Mac's physical address space[1]. The source code of Mac OS X kernel is freely available from Apple Open Source connection [5] and

---

[1] 4GiB limitation is caused by the 32-bit addressing of the host memory used in FireWire.

together with the debugging symbol information available in Apple's Kernel debugging kits, it can be used to interpret the content of the accessible Apple Mac RAM.

The method for interpreting the content of physical memory dumps of Apple Mac computers was first described by M. Suiche in [6]. In particular, it was shown that the virtual address of the *statically* allocated data structures in Mac OS X kernel is equal to the corresponding physical memory address. In relation to FireWire RAM imaging this means that if, for example, a statically allocated kernel data structure has virtual address 0x005db044, it can be accessed over FireWire using physical address 0x005db044. This rule does not apply to all kernel data, but it does apply to all data structures mentioned in this paper.

The address of the statically allocated data structure in a particular version of Mac OS X can be determined by examining its kernel executable file `mach_kernel` using, for example, nm command as shown in Fig. 1.

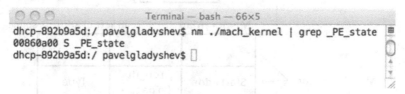

Fig. 1. Determining the address of a kernel data structure

The kernel executable files for different versions of Mac OS X can be downloaded from the Apple Developer Connection [7] as part of the kernel debugging kits.

Determining the Version of Mac OS X. Mac OS X kernel has a string constant called `version`, which is a null-terminated ASCII string describing the version of Mac OS X. E.g. "Darwin Kernel Version 10.0.0: Fri Jul 31 22:47:34 PDT 2009; ...". The address of the `version` string is different in different versions of Mac OS X.

The version of Mac OS X running on the target computer can be determined by reading the contents of every possible location of the `version` string over FireWire and comparing the acquired data with the expected content of the `version` string. Once the `version` string for a particular version of Mac OS X is found at its expected location, it can be concluded that that version of Mac OS X is running on the target computer.

Determining Safe Memory Regions for Imaging. Intel-based Apple Mac computers implement Extendible Firmware Interface (EFI) standard [8]. According to the EFI specification, computer firmware communicates the layout of memory mapped I/O registers and other areas of memory to the operating system at boot time. Mac OS X stores this information in the kernel and uses it when the computer is put to sleep to determine all memory areas whose content needs to be saved onto the hard disk. This information is stored in the `MemoryMap` data structure, whose address can be determined via FireWire by reading `PE_state` and `boot_args` kernel data structures as illustrated in Fig. 2.

`PE_state` is a global data structure in Mac OS X kernel that contains data of the Platform Expert object. It is defined in the file `pexpert/pexpert/pexpert.h` in the kernel source code tree:

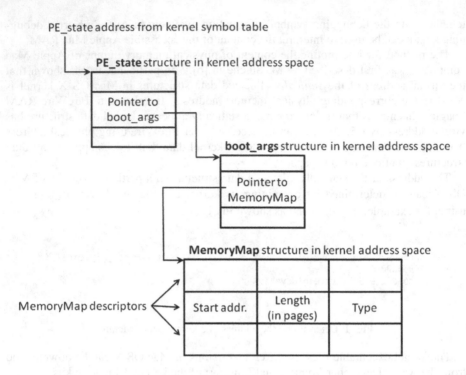

Fig. 2. Accessing Mac OS X memory map

```
typedef struct PE_state {
        boolean_t initialized;
        PE_Video video;
        void *deviceTreeHead;
        void *bootArgs;
} PE_state_t;
```

Among other things, the PE_state structure contains a pointer called bootArgs, which points to the boot arguments passed to the kernel by the firmware at the boot time.

The boot arguments are organized into a struct called boot_args, which is defined in the file pexpert/pexpert/i386/boot.h:

```
typedef struct boot_args {
   uint16_t    Revision;
   uint16_t    Version;
   char        CommandLine[BOOT_LINE_LENGTH];
   uint32_t    MemoryMap;
   uint32_t    MemoryMapSize;
   uint32_t    MemoryMapDescriptorSize;
   uint32_t    MemoryMapDescriptorVersion;
   ...
} boot_args;
```

One of `boot_args` fields, `MemoryMap`, is a pointer to the memory map of the computer. The memory map is an array of memory map descriptors, where each descriptor defines the location, type, and size of a particular area of memory. A memory map descriptor has the following structure (defined in `pexpert/pexpert/i386/boot.h`):

```
typedef struct EfiMemoryRange {
    uint32_t Type;
    uint32_t Pad;
    uint64_t PhysicalStart;
    uint64_t VirtualStart;
    uint64_t NumberOfPages;
    uint64_t Attribute;
} EfiMemoryRange;
```

The `Type` field determines the purpose of the area of memory (e.g. normal RAM vs. memory mapped I/O registers). The `PhysicalStart` field contains the physical address of where the memory area begins. The `NumberOfPages` determines the length of the memory area in pages.

The address of `PE_state` data structure can be determined from the kernel symbol table. The offsets to `bootArgs` and `MemoryMap` pointers can be calculated by adding up sizes of the preceding fields in the `PE_state` and `boot_args` data structures respectively.

Once the RAM imaging application has determined the version of Mac OS X in the target computer, it must use the address of `PE_state` and offsets to `bootArgs` and `MemoryMap` pointers for that version of Mac OS X. To determine which areas of memory are safe for reading, the RAM imaging application should perform a sweep of the memory map array and identify all memory areas corresponding to some form of RAM. The content of the identified RAM areas should then be acquired via FireWire.

After the RAM image is created, it needs to be analyzed. This paper describes a work in progress whose aim is the recovery of unsaved instant messenger conversations from the RAM of the target computer. Some initial results for recovery of AOL Instant Messenger (AIM) conversation fragments have been obtained, and they are described in the next section.

3 Extracting Fragments of Open AIM Conversations

3.1 AOL Instant Messenger Background

AOL Instant Messenger (AIM) is a peer-to-peer instant messaging service similar to many other "chat" type programs. Below are some of the features and services AIM provides:

- A user can have up to 1000 buddies added to his/her contact list.
- Ability to add, delete or block any buddies in buddy list.
- Viewing buddy information and knowing his/her details.
- A user can also send typed text messages to many buddies at a time.

- The ability to share a user's status, files and pictures.
- The ability to use Text (SMS). This feature sends instant messages to the recipient's cell phone.
- AOL provides a free email account.
- AIM toolbar provides the ability to see the status of AOL mail, AOL search functions, and AIM messaging services as a toolbar in your browser.
- In addition AIM is accessible on Windows Mobile Smartphone, iPhone and iPod touch [3].

Due to its availability, features, and ease of use AIM has become very popular.

By default, the Mac OS X version of AIM does not automatically save chat logs. This is a hindrance from an investigative point of view. To obtain the content of an AIM conversation an investigator needs to extract it from RAM. Section 2 covers this.

3.2 AOL Instant Messenger Chat Logs Formats in the RAM

The research described in this paper focused on AIM version 1.5.127. To determine formats of conversation data as stored in RAM, a test conversation was conducted. The content of the virtual memory of the AIM process was then dumped using gcore-1.3 [4], and the resulting virtual memory dump was then examined using hexadecimal editor 0xED [11]. As a result of this experimentation, several possible AIM message formats were discovered. These formats and the recovery of chat logs are described in the following sections.

Format A

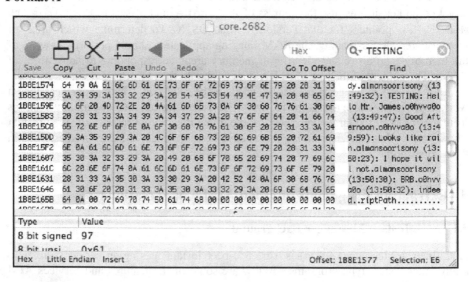

Fig. 3. AIM chat log format A

By searching for known conversation fragments, it was possible to locate conversation data objects in RAM (Fig. 3). From the AIM process memory dump, it can be seen that AIM chat messages have the following format. It contains the user name of the sender, the time when the message was sent, and the text of the message:

```
<USERNAME> (HH:MM:SS): <MESSAGE>
```

The username can only be 3-16 combined letters and numbers, but it should always start with an upper or lower case letter. Given below is a regular expression written in Perl that matches the above message format:

```
m/([a-zA-Z]{1}[a-zA-Z0-
9]{2,15})\s\((\d\d\:\d\d:\d\d)\):\s(.*\s)/
```

Format B. However, after further research it was found that the RAM sometimes contains a different format for the AIM messages, an example of which is shown in Fig. 4.

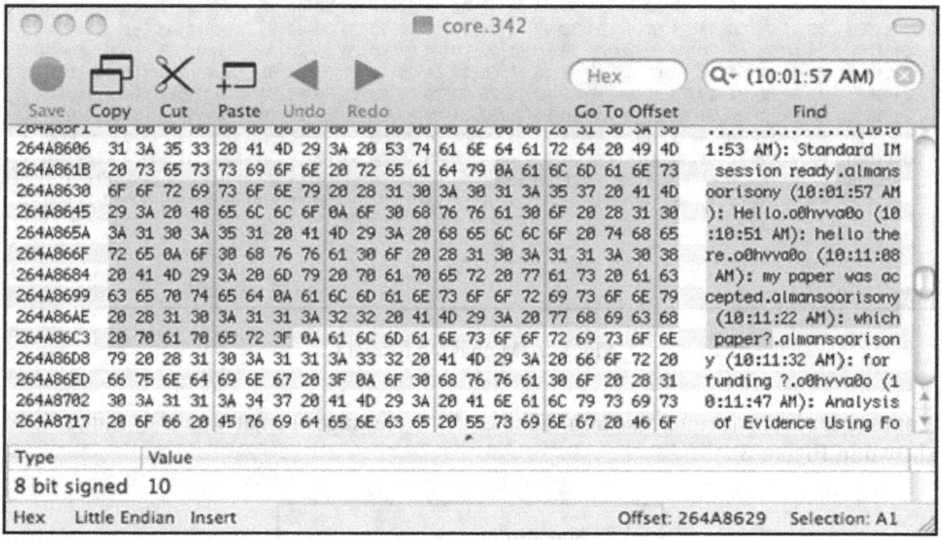

Fig. 4. AIM chat log format B

From Fig. 4 the messages format is:

```
<USERNAME> (HH:MM:SS PM/AM): <MESSAGE>
```

In Perl matching the above chat message format would be the following expression:

```
m/([a-zA-Z]{1}[a-zA-Z0-
9]{2,15})\s(\(\d\d\:\d\d:\d\d\s[A-Z]{2}\):)\s(.*\s)/
```

Format C. Another format for AIM chat logs was also found that has the following format:

```
<USERNAME>: (HH:MM:SS) <MESSAGE>
```

To extract this chat message format the following regular expression in Perl can be used:

```
m/([a-zA-Z]{1}[a-zA-Z0-
9]{2,15}:)\s(\(\d\d\:\d\d:\d\d\))(.*\s)/
```

See Fig. 5 for the above AIM chat log format.

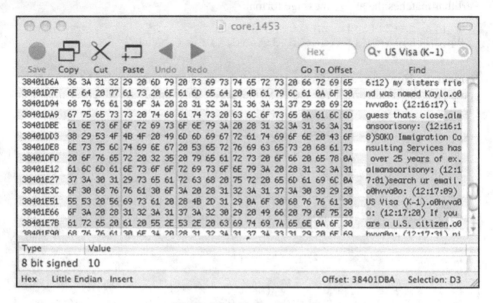

Fig. 5. AIM chat log format C

Format D. From further research, another AIM message format was also found. It is shown in Figure 6.

\\df2 \ almansoorisony

\\bs1 \\bf2

\\bs3 \\bf2 \ Good evening my friend

Fig. 6. AIM chat log format D

The name of the sender (almansoorisony) and the text of the message (Good evening my friend) can be extracted using, for example, the following Perl code:

```
if (m/\\[a-z0-9]{3}\s([a-zA-Z]{1}[a-zA-Z0-9]{2,15}:).*/){
    $username = $1;
    my $firstline = <FILE>;
    $secondline = <FILE>;          #Skip \\bs1 \\bf2
    $secondline =~ m/[^\s]*\s(.*)/;
    $secondline = $1;
    $conversation2 = "$username $secondline";
}
```

The above code will extract the username, assign it to the variable $username, and then extract the conversation fragments from the following two lines read from the memory dump file according to the format displayed in Fig. 6.

4 Experimental Results

The techniques described in Sections 2 and 3 have been implemented in a software tool called Goldfish [9]. The tool has been tested on three distinct Apple Mac computers, which were using one of the two different versions of Mac OS X (Darwin Kernel Version 10.0.0 and Darwin Kernel Version 9.8.0). Results have been mixed; in all experiments the tool successfully performed RAM imaging over FireWire without crashing the target computer. In most experiments AIM messages of the ongoing AIM conversations were successfully recovered. However, in some experiments, AIM message recovery did not recover any messages. The reasons for this failure to recover messages are being investigated.

5 Future Work

The research described in this paper is a work in progress. The basic method for extracting RAM content from Apple Mac computers over FireWire has been developed, and the initial steps in the analysis of the RAM dump were performed.

Future work will have to focus on further analysis of the RAM dump. In order to go beyond the simple data carving using regular expressions, it will be necessary to reconstruct the virtual memory spaces of the individual user processes. A method for doing so has been proposed in [6]. Additional difficulty is caused by the inconsistencies in the RAM dump. RAM imaging over FireWire is a lengthy process that happens concurrently with the normal operation of the target computer. As a result, the content of some memory pages may have changed during the imaging process, and the data collected at the beginning of the imaging may contradict the data collected at the end of the imaging. The future research will have to come up with a way of identifying and working around such inconsistencies.

References

1. Boileau, A.: Hit by Bus: Physical Access Attacks with Firewire,
   http://www.security-assessment.com/nz/publications/
   security_publications.html
2. Boileau, A.: Releases: Winlockpwd, Pythonraw1394-1.0.tar.gz,
   http://www.storm.net.nz/projects/16
3. Wikipedia Article: AOL Instant Messenger,
   http://en.wikipedia.org/wiki/AOL_Instant_Messenger
4. Singh, A.: Process Photography on Mac OS X (Handcrafting Process Core Dumps),
   http://www.osxbook.com/book/bonus/chapter8/core
5. Apple Open Source Connection, http://opensource.apple.com/

6. Suiche, M.: Advanced Mac OS X memory analysis, Presentation at BlackHat Briefing Washington DC (February 2010), http://www.blackhat.com/presentations/bh-dc-10/Suiche_Matthieu/Blackhat-DC-2010-Advanced-Mac-OS-X-Physical-Memory-Analysis-wp.pdf
7. Apple Developer Connection, http://developer.apple.com/
8. Unified Extendible Firmware Interface Specifications, http://www.uefi.org/specs
9. Goldfish tool, http://cci.ucd.ie/goldfish
10. Becher, M., Dornseif, M., Klein, C.N.: 0wn3d by an iPod. In: Proceedings of PacSec 2004 Applied Security Conference, Tokyo (2004), http://pacsec.jp/psj04/psj04-dornseif-e.ppt
11. 0xED hexadecimal editor, http://www.suavetech.com/0xed/0xed.html

Towards More Secure Biometric Readers
for Effective Digital Forensic Investigation

Zouheir Trabelsi[1], Mohamed Al-Hemairy[2], Ibrahim Baggili[3], and Saad Amin[4]

[1] Faculty of Information Technology
[2] Research Affairs Sector,
UAE University, Al Ain, P.O. Box 17551, UAE
{trabelsi,m.hussien}@uaeu.ac.ae
[3] College of Information Technology, Advanced Cyber Forensics Research Laboratory
Zayed University, Abu Dhabi, UAE
Ibrahim.Baggili@zu.ac.ae
[4] College of Informatics, British University in Dubai,
Dubai, P.O. Box 502216, UAE
Saad.Amin@BUiD.ac.ae

Abstract. This paper investigates the effect of common network attacks on the performance, and security of several biometric readers. Experiments are conducted using Denial of Service attacks (DoSs) and the ARP cache poisoning attack. The experiments show that the tested biometric readers are vulnerable to DoS attacks, and their recognition performance is significantly affected after launching the attacks. However, the experiments show that the tested biometric readers are secure from the ARP cache poisoning attack. This work demonstrates that biometric readers are easy targets for malicious network users, lack basic security mechanisms, and are vulnerable to common attacks. The confidentiality, and integrity of the log files in the biometric readers, could be compromised with such attacks. It then becomes important to study these attacks in order to find flags that could aid in a network forensic investigation of a biometric device.

Keywords: Fingerprint reader, Iris reader, Biometrics scanners, Denial of Service attack (DoS), forensic investigation, Firewall, Intrusion Detection/Prevention Systems (IDS/IPS).

1 Introduction

Digital forensic investigations focus on finding digital evidence after a computer or network security incident has occurred, or locating data from systems that may form part of some litigation, even if it is deleted. The goal of digital forensics is to perform a structured investigation to find out what happened on the digital system, and who was responsible for it.

Nowadays, many networks include biometric readers, such as fingerprint, face and iris readers, used for user identification and verification, in addition to the common network devices (computers, servers, switches, routers and firewalls). These readers

I. Baggili (Ed.): ICDF2C 2010, LNICST 53, pp. 65–77, 2011.

exchange biometric data with remote servers via networks. In case of incidents, the readers' logs and the biometric data may be used by digital forensic investigators to acquire digital evidence. However, insecure and vulnerable biometric readers may not contribute in finding exactly what happened on the digital systems. Therefore, prior to any digital investigation, it is important that digital forensic investigators have sufficient knowledge about the security level of the biometric readers, and the data involved in the investigation.

This paper focuses on investigating the security of some biometric readers, and the corresponding exchanged biometric data. Precisely, we investigate the effect of common network attacks on the performance and security of the biometric readers. Experiments are conducted using DoS attacks and ARP cache poisoning attack, and they are part of a master thesis submitted to the British University in Dubai (BUiD), School of Informatics, in partial fulfillment of the requirements for the degree of M.Sc. in Information and Networking Security.

2 Biometric Technologies

In 2001 MIT Technology Review [7] named biometrics as one of the "top ten emerging technologies that will change the world". The term "Biometric" comes from the Greek words "bio" (life) and "metric" (to measure). Biometric refers to technologies used for measuring and analyzing a person's unique characteristics. There are two types of biometrics: behavioral and physical. Behavioral biometrics are generally used for verification while physical biometrics can be used for either identification or verification.

Identification is determining who a person is. It involves trying to find a match for a person's biometric data in a database containing records of biometric information about people. This method requires time and a large amount of processing power, especially if the database is large. Verification is determining if a person is who he/she say he/she really is. It involves comparing a user's biometric data to the previously recorded data for that person to ensure that this is the same person. This method requires less processing power and time, and is usually used for authentication and access control.

The most common types of biometric technologies are fingerprint, iris, voice, hand geometry, and face recognition [1, 2, 3, 9]. Each technology has its own benefits and challenges. Today, fingerprint and iris technologies are widely used [10] because they are fast, reliable, stable, cost effective, and provide excellent identification accuracy rates. Iris recognition is the most precise of all biometric identification systems. The false acceptance ratio is so low that the probability of falsely identifying one individual as another is virtually zero [8].

Biometric technologies may seem trendy, but their use is becoming increasingly common. Currently, biometric readers are deployed in many public sites and are used for user identification and verification. They play an important role in implementing security policies within the institutions. Most biometric readers are able to connect to local area networks (LAN), and communicate with remote biometric servers to exchange biometric data.

Biometric reader manufacturers have been focusing on offering easy to use, practical devices, with low cost, low enrollment and recognition time, and low rate of false match and non-match. However, since these devices are as any network host with IP and MAC addresses and may be targets of malicious network users.

3 Network Attacks

DoS attacks and the ARP cache poisoning attack [11] are the two classes of network attacks that are used in this research. Mainly, two experiments have been conducted. In the first experiment, we investigate the effect of DoS attacks on the performance of fingerprint, and iris readers. In the second experiment, we investigate the ability of ARP cache poisoning attack to corrupt the ARP cache entries of the biometrics readers. Network hosts with corrupted ARP caches may not be able to communicate properly with the other network hosts.

3.1 DoS Attacks

A DoS is an attack which attempts to render a system unusable or significantly slow down the system for legitimate users by overloading the resources so no one else can access it. A DoS attack may target users, preventing them from establishing outgoing connections on a network. A DoS attack may also target an entire organization, to either prevent outgoing traffic or to prevent incoming traffic to certain network services, such as an organization's web page.

DoS attacks are much easier to accomplish than remotely gaining administrative access to a target system. Because of this, DoS attacks have become common on the Internet. DoS attacks can either be deliberate or accidental. It is caused deliberately when an unauthorized user actively overloads a resource. It is caused accidentally when an authorized user unintentionally performs an action that causes resources to become unavailable.

Most DoS attacks rely on weaknesses in the TCP/IP protocols. The next subsections introduce the selected DoS attacks used in this paper's experiments, namely the SYN flood, Land, Teardrop and UDP flood attacks.

Land Attack: Land attack occurs when an attacker sends spoofed TCP SYN packets (connection initiation) with the target host's IP address, and an open port as both source and destination. The target host responds by sending the SYN-ACK packet to itself, creating an empty connection that lasts until the idle timeout value is reached. Flooding a system with such empty connections can overwhelm the system, causing a DoS (Figure 1).

SYN Flood Attack: A SYN flood occurs when a host becomes so overwhelmed by SYN packets initiating incomplete connection requests that it can no longer process legitimate connection requests.

When a client system attempts to establish a TCP connection to a system providing a service (the server), the client, and server exchange a sequence set of messages known as a three-way handshake.

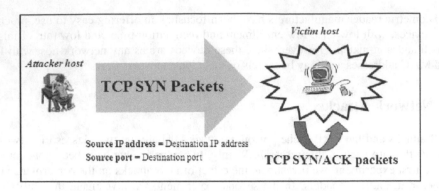

Fig. 1. The Land attack

The client system begins by sending a SYN (synchronization) message to the server. The server then acknowledges the SYN message by sending a SYN-ACK (acknowledgment) message to the client. The client then finishes establishing the connection by responding with an ACK message. The connection between the client and the server is then opened, and the service-specific data can be exchanged between the client and the server.

The potential for abuse arises at the point where the server system has sent an acknowledgment (SYN-ACK) back to the client, but it has not yet received the final ACK message. This is what is known as a half-opened connection. The server has in its system memory a built-in data structure describing all pending connections. This data structure is of finite size, and it can be made to overflow by intentionally creating too many partially-opened connections (Figure 2).

Creating a half–opened connection is easily accomplished with IP spoofing. The attacker's system sends SYN messages to the victim's server that appear to be legitimate, but in fact, the source address is spoofed to a system that is not currently connected to the network. This means that the final ACK message is never sent to the victim server. Because the source address is spoofed, there is no way to determine the identity of the true attacker when the packet arrives at the victim's system.

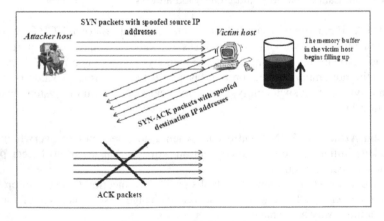

Fig. 2. The SYN Flood attack

Teardrop Attack: The Teardrop attack targets a vulnerability in the way fragmented IP packets are reassembled. Fragmentation is necessary when IP datagrams are larger than the maximum transmission unit (MTU) of a network segment across which the datagrams must traverse. In order to successfully reassemble packets at the receiving end, the IP header for each fragment includes an offset to identify the fragment's position in the original unfragmented packet. In a Teardrop attack, packet fragments are deliberately fabricated with overlapping offset fields causing the host to hang or crash when it tries to reassemble them. Figure 3 shows that the second fragment packet claims to begin 20 bytes earlier (at 800) than the first fragment packet ends (at 820). The offset of fragment Packet #2 is not in accord with the packet length of fragment Packet #1. This discrepancy can cause some systems to crash during the reassembly attempt.

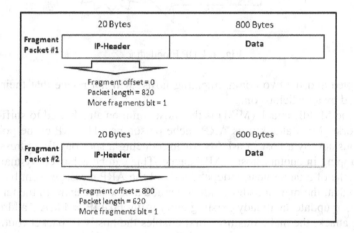

Fig. 3. The Teardrop attack

UDP Flood Attack: UDP (User Datagram Protocol) is a connectionless protocol, and it does not require any connection set up procedure to transfer data. A UDP Flood attack is possible when an attacker sends a UDP packet to a random port on the victim system. When the victim system receives a UDP packet, it will determine what application is waiting on the destination UDP port. Two cases are possible. If there is no application that is waiting on the port (closed UDP port), the victim host will generate an ICMP (Internet Control Message Protocol) packet of destination unreachable to the forged source address. However, if there is an application running on the destination UDP port, then the application will handle the UDP packet. In both cases, if enough UDP packets are delivered to destination UDP ports, the victim host or application may slow down or go down (Figure 4).

3.2 ARP Cache Poisoning Attack

Sniffing consists of re-routing (redirecting) the network traffic between two target hosts to a malicious host. Then, the malicious host will forward the received packets to the original destination; so that the communication between the two target hosts is

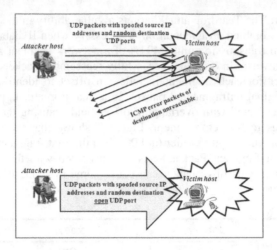

Fig. 4. UDP Flood attack

not interrupted and the two communicating hosts' will not notice that their traffic is being sniffed by a malicious one.

Man-in-the-Middle attack (MiM) is the most common attack used to sniff switched LAN networks. MiM attack uses ARP cache poisoning[11]. ARP cache poisoning is the malicious act, by a host in a LAN, of introducing a spurious IP address to MAC address mapping in another host's ARP cache. This can be achieved by manipulating the ARP cache of a target host, independently of the ARP messages sent by the target host. To do that, the malicious host can either add a new fake entry in the target host's ARP cache, or update an already existing entry using fake IP and MAC addresses.

In MiM attack, the malicious user first enables the host's IP packet routing, in order to become a router and forward the redirected packets. Then, using an ARP cache poisoning attack, the malicious user corrupts the ARP caches of the two target hosts in order to force the two hosts to forward all their packets. It is important to notice that if the malicious host corrupts the ARP caches of the two target hosts without enabling its IP packet routing, then the two hosts will not be able to exchange packets, and it will be a DoS attack. In this case, the malicious host does not forward the received packets to their legitimate destination as shown in Figure 5.

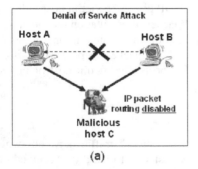
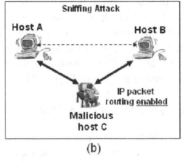

Fig. 5. Biometric data sniffing based on the MiM attack

4   Experiments

Two experiments are conducted. In the first experiment [14], we investigate the effect of four common DoS attacks on the performance of several fingerprint and iris readers. In the second experiment, we investigate the effect of ARP cache poisoning attack on the entries of the ARP caches of the biometric readers.

4.1   Network Architecture

Figure 6 shows the network architecture used in the experiments. Three attacker hosts, a biometric server, fingerprint readers, and iris readers are connected to a switch. The attacks are lunched from the three attack hosts using two tools.

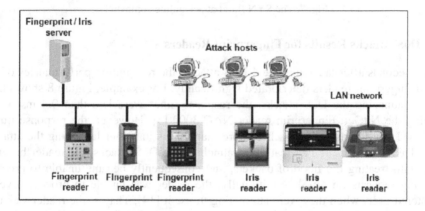

Fig. 6. Network architecture

4.2   Attack Tools

The following are the two tools used in the experiments [14]:

- FrameIP packet generator [12] is a packet generator that allows generating any type of IP and ARP packets. The tool is used by the attack hosts to generate the Land, Teardrop, and UDP flood attacks; it is also used to perform an ARP cache poisoning attack.
- SYNFlood tool [13] is a ready-to-use attack tool used to generate the SYN flood attack.

Figure 7 show the online command used to generate the SYN flood attack, using the tool SYNflood. After executing the online command, a flood of fake TCP SYN packets is sent to the target biometric reader whose IP address is 10.10.10.5.

Using the three attack hosts, SYN flood, Land, Teardrop and UDP flood attacks are lunched simultaneously. The following section presents the experimental results.

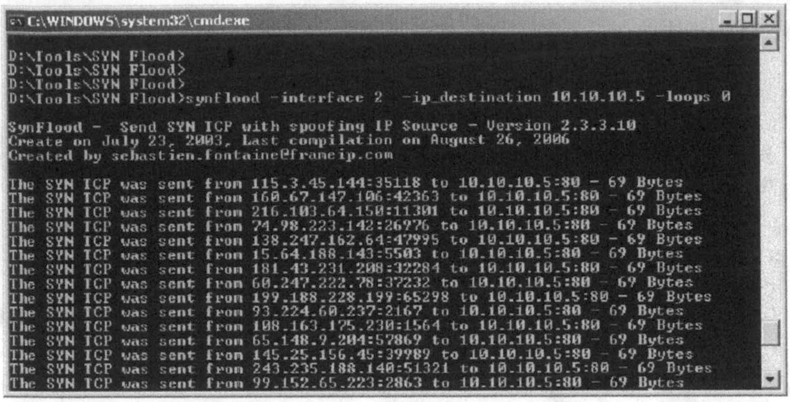

Fig. 7. The SYN flood attack online command

4.3 DoS Attacks Results for Fingerprint Readers

A few seconds after launching the 4 DoS attacks, the recognition performances of all tested fingerprint readers deteriorated significantly. For example, Figure 8 shows that before launching the DoS attacks, the response times were less than 0.4 ms when pinging the NitGen Fingerprint reader NAC 3000 [5]. However, the response times increased considerably and reached more than 20 ms just after launching the attacks [14]. This is due to the fact that after launching the DoS attacks, the reader became busy with treating the flood of packets, and consequently became unable to process the Ping requests on time.   Additionally, the reader was unable to process several registered users when they were attempting to use it [14]. That is, the reader was unable to give any recognition results. Table 1 summarizes the experimental results for each fingerprint reader.

Table 1. DoS attacks results for fingerprint readers

	Effect of DoS attacks on the recognition performance of the fingerprint readers
NitGen Fingerprint reader NAC 3000 (http://www.nitgen.com)	Recognition status is unstable: • The reader recognition response is very slow or there is no response.
F7 Standalone Biometric Access Control Terminal (http://www.fslocks.com/f7stbiaccote.html)	
MX600 Fingerprint Access Control (http://www.miaxis.net/1070012/1/products_details.htm)	• The readers often disconnect from the network.

4.4 DoS Attacks Results for Iris Readers

In this experiment [14], the iris readers are the targets of the attack hosts. The same four DoS attacks are used in this experiment. A few seconds after launching the DoS attacks, the recognition performances of all tested iris readers deteriorated significantly. Table 2 summarizes the experiments results for each iris reader [14].

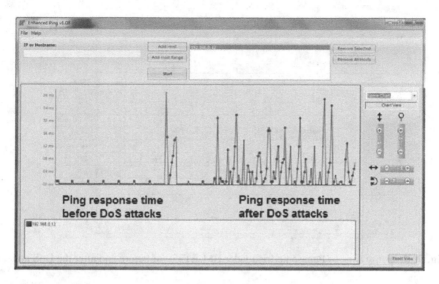

Fig. 8. Response time of Nitgen Fingerprint reader NAC 3000 before and after the DoS attacks

Table 2. DoS attacks results for iris readers

	Effect of DoS attacks on the recognition performance of the iris readers
Panasonic Iris reader BM-ET330 (ftp://ftp.panasonic.com/pub/Panasonic/cctv/SpecS heets/BM-ET330.pdf)	Recognition status is unstable: -The reader recognition response is very slow or there is no response.
LG's IrisAccess 4000 (http://www.irisid.com)	-The readers disconnected from the network. But, when the DoS attack stopped, the readers reconnected to the network.
IG-AD100® Iris Camera System, **(http://www.irisguard.com)**	

For example, Figure 9 shows that before launching the DoS attacks, the response times were less than 0.1 ms when pinging the Panasonic Iris reader BM-ET330 [4]. However, just after launching the attacks, the reader crashed, and consequently there were no ping responses. The reader became unable to recognize users and completely disconnected from the network. When the DoS attack stopped, the reader reconnected to the network [14].

4.5 ARP Cache Poisoning Attack Results for Fingerprint and Iris Readers

This attack consists of corrupting the ARP caches of the biometric readers. Network hosts with corrupted ARP caches may not be able to communicate properly with other network hosts.

We use the FrameIP packet generator tool to build fake ARP packets [14]. The packets are used to corrupt the ARP caches of the fingerprint and iris readers. Figure 10 shows the online command used to generate the fake ARP packets.

The experimental results indicate that the ARP cache poisoning attack has no effect on the tested readers. Consequently, the readers are protected from this type of attack. This is because of the simple implementation of the ARP protocol in these readers. In fact, the readers do not allow the updating of their ARP caches [14]. They use static

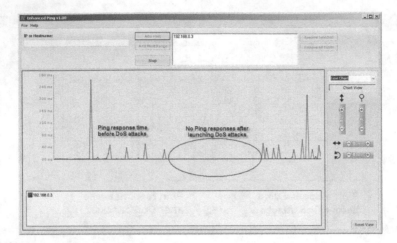

Fig. 9. Response time of Panasonic Iris reader BM-ET330 of before and after the DoS attacks

```
C:\WINDOWS\system32\cmd.exe                                           _ □ ×
D:\Tools\frame_ip>
D:\Tools\frame_ip>
D:\Tools\frame_ip>
D:\Tools\frame_ip>frameip -interface 2 -mac_type 2054 -arp_ip_source 192.168.0.2
 -arp_mac_source 01-01-01-01-01-01 -arp_ip_destination 192.168.0.10

FrameIP - Create some IP frame - Version 5.9.3.12
Create on December 21, 2002, Last compilation on March 13, 2007
Created by Sebastien FONTAINE - http://www.frameip.com

The frame was sent from 00-19-7E-8C-32-03 to FF-FF-FF-FF-FF-FF with 57 Bytes

D:\Tools\frame_ip>_
```

Fig. 10. FrameIP online command used to perform ARP cache poisoning attack

ARP cache entries, so that the entries cannot be updated by fake ARP request and replies. The ARP cache entries are created when the readers connect to the network. Once they get the MAC addresses of the biometric servers, they create static entries (IP/MAC addresses) in their ARP caches.

5   Enhanced Network Architecture for e-Forensic Investigation

In case of incident, forensic investigators need to collect, and analyze the data exchanged between the network devices (routers, firewalls, intrusions detection systems, etc.), including the biometric readers and the servers. This investigation allows to propose a more enhanced configuration for a network that includes biometric readers. The log files of the network devices and biometric readers should be collected to be used in any investigation. In addition, sniffers should be installed in order to collect the exchanged traffic between the devices. A host running a sniffer, and connected to a network will not be able to sniff the traffic, unless it is connect to a monitoring port (SPAN), Figure 11. A host connect to a SPAN port will receive all the network traffic exchanged between all the network devices. Hence, forensic investigators can use the

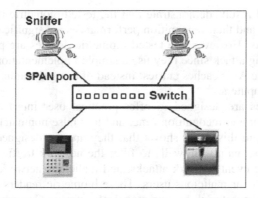

Fig. 11. A network architecture with SPAN port for sniffing network traffic

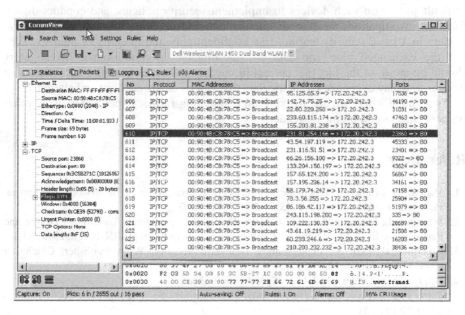

Fig. 12. CommView sniffer showing traffic generated by SYN flood attack

sniffed traffic to start their investigation in case of incidents. For example, Figure 12, shows the collected SYN flood attack traffic using the CommView sniffer. By investigating the collected traffic, it is clear that host 172.20.243.3 has been under SYN flood attack.

6 Conclusion

This paper investigated the effect of common network attacks on the performance and security of several fingerprint and iris readers. Experiments were conducted using DoS attacks and ARP cache poisoning attacks.

The experimental results demonstrate that the tested biometric readers are vulnerable to DoS attacks, and their recognition performances are significantly affected after launching the attacks. However, the tested biometric devices are protected from the ARP cache poisoning attack since they use a simple implementation of the ARP protocol. They use static ARP caches entries; instead of using dynamic entries as it is the case in ordinary computers.

Biometric devices are designed to offer practical user interfaces with effective costs, low enrollment and recognition time, and low false nonmatch and match rates. However, our work in this paper shows that they are not designed to include basic security mechanisms, mainly firewalls to filter the network traffic and IDS/IPS systems to detect and prevent network attacks, and malicious network activities. Therefore, they are targets for malicious users. These biometric readers can be crashed or disconnected from the network by common DoS attacks. Consequently, their availability and efficiency may become questionable within any institution, and it will be difficult to rely on such devices to implement security policies, and conduct digital forensic investigations in case of an incident. Furthermore, since these biometric readers lack basic security features, the confidentiality and integrity of their log files and the exchanged biometric data are questionable. Digital forensic investigators should be aware of the fact that current biometric readers are insecure and vulnerable devices and may exchange biometric data that can be easily attacked and altered.

As a future work, we are working on conducting further experiments using other types of attacks and biometric readers.

References

1. Vacca, J.: Biometric Technologies and Verification Systems. Butterworth-Heinemann Publisher, Butterworths (2007) ISBN-10: 0750679670
2. Wayman, J., Jain, A., Maltoni, D., Maio, D.: Biometric Systems: Technology Design and Performance Evaluation. Springer Publisher, Heidelberg (2004) ISBN-10: 1852335963
3. Chirillo, J., Blaul, S.: Implementing Biometric Security. Wiley Publisher, Chichester (2003) ISBN-10: 0764525026
4. Panasonic Iris reader BM-ET330, Specification Sheet,
   ftp://ftp.panasonic.com/pub/Panasonic/cctv/SpecSheets/
   BM-ET330.pdf
5. Nitgen Fingerprint reader NAC 3000, Specification Sheet, http://www.nitgen.com
6. Daugman, J.: Recognising Persons by Their Iris Patterns. In: Li, S.Z., Lai, J.-H., Tan, T., Feng, G.-C., Wang, Y. (eds.) SINOBIOMETRICS 2004. LNCS, vol. 3338, pp. 5–25. Springer, Heidelberg (2004)
7. The MIT Technology Review in the Emerging Technologies That Will Change the World, Ten emerging technologies that will change the world (January/February 2001),
   http://www.techreview.com
8. Duagman, J.: How Iris Recognition Works. IEEE Transactions on Circuits and Systems for Video Technology 14, 21–30 (2004)
9. Tony, M.: Biometric authentication in the real world, Centre for Mathematics and Scientific Computing, National Physical Laboratory, UK (Online) (2001),
   http://www.npl.co.uk/upload/pdf/biometrics_psrevho.pdf

10. Al-Raisi, A., Al-Khouri, A.: Iris Recognition and the Challenge of Homeland and Border Control Security in UAE. Journal of Telematics and Informatics 25, 117–132 (2008)
11. Trabelsi, Z., Shuaib, K.: A Novel Man-in-the-Middle Intrusion Detection Scheme for Switched LANs. The International Journal of Computers and Applications 3(3) (2008)
12. FrameIP Packet Generator, http://www.FrameIP.com
13. SYN flood, http://www.FrameIP.com
14. Al-Hemairy, M., Trabelsi, Z., Amin, S.: Sniffing Attacks Prevention/Detection Techniques in LAN networks & the effect on Biometric Technology. A thesis submitted to The British University in Dubai, School of Informatics (May 2010)

Defining a Standard for Reporting Digital Evidence Items in Computer Forensic Tools

Hamda Bariki, Mariam Hashmi, and Ibrahim Baggili

Advanced Cyber Forensics Research Laboratory
College of Information Technology
Zayed University, Abu Dhabi, UAE
Ibrahim.Baggili@zu.ac.ae

Abstract. Due to the lack of standards in reporting digital evidence items, investigators are facing difficulties in efficiently presenting their findings. This paper proposes a standard for digital evidence to be used in reports that are generated using computer forensic software tools. The authors focused on developing a standard digital evidence items by surveying various digital forensic tools while keeping in mind the legal integrity of digital evidence items. Additionally, an online questionnaire was used to gain the opinion of knowledgeable and experienced stakeholders in the digital forensics domain. Based on the findings, the authors propose a standard for digital evidence items that includes data about the case, the evidence source, evidence item, and the chain of custody. Research results enabled the authors in creating a defined XML schema for digital evidence items.

Keywords: digital evidence item, reports in forensic tools, digital forensics, standard report.

1 Introduction

Today, digital forensics plays a critical role in investigations. The broad use of digital devices in daily life activities make them an important source of information about people, thus causing them to become a strong potential source of evidence. Anson and Bunting (2007) claimed that if an incident takes place, one of the most important sources of evidence will be the digital devices at the scene. Investigators are using digital forensics to extract digital evidence from electronic devices. Digital forensics typically follows a four step process, which includes: acquisition, identification, evaluation, and presentation as shown in Figure 1 (Anson & Bunting, 2007). This research focused on the last step of digital forensics process, which is presentation.

Practitioners may need to present their investigative findings to courts of law. Typically, investigators include their findings on digital evidence items, which are known as data objects associated with such digital evidence at the time of acquisition or seizure (Anson & Bunting, 2007). Digital evidence items comprise a myriad of computer based data, such as word documents, jpeg files, or any data that could reside on a storage medium. Some digital forensics software tools implement a reporting functionality which allows forensic examiners to generate reports regarding digital

I. Baggili (Ed.): ICDF2C 2010, LNICST 53, pp. 78–95, 2011.

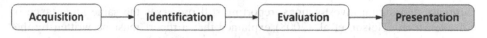

Fig. 1. Digital forensics process

evidence items found. Reports generated from forensic tools are sometimes included with the official investigation report that is presented to attorneys.

2 Problem Statement

Nowadays, investigators typically use multiple computer forensic tools during their investigation process to verify their findings, and cover all possible evidence items. For that reason, as shown in Figure 2, investigators may end up with multiple reports on digital evidence items, generated using different tools. The lack of standards in the reporting function of computer forensic tools may hinder the computer investigation process. When an investigator uses different forensic tools, he/she may face difficulties in integrating evidence items from software-generated reports into the official investigation report that could be presented to attorneys or clients.

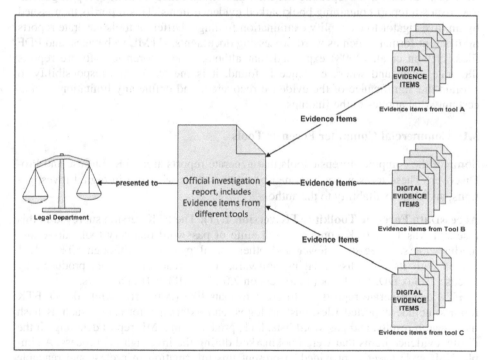

Fig. 2. Digital investigation report

3 Related Literature and Software

Reporting is critical in any investigation. It is the method for communicating information about the results, and findings of the investigation process. When it comes to computer and digital investigations, reporting still preserves the same importance if not even more. Nelson et al. (2008) explained that a report must be written by the forensic examiner to illustrate the findings from a digital forensics examination. In this report, the examiner needs to explain his investigation process, and findings. This report can be used to present evidence in the court, or to support issuing a search warrant. It can also be used to communicate expert opinion.

To perform computer forensic tasks, one needs software tools to gain access, and uncover information that is not clearly visible such as files that are deleted, stored in slack space or unallocated space, and files that are hidden or encrypted. Furthermore, many tools may be needed to perform investigative tasks such as forensic imaging, searching, documenting, decrypting and much more, which are needed to success-fully, critically, and correctly analyze digital storage media. With many computer forensic software tools, such as FTK, ProDiscover, iLook, and EnCase, log files and reports are generated when performing an investigation. These reports could be at-tached to an official investigation report that is presented to the attorney. The content and the format of these reports will not be the same.

Log reports record the activities the investigator performed during the examination, which can be useful for repeating the examination if needed. A built-in report genera-tor creates a report containing bookmarked evidence items. This report is then issued by an investigator to exemplify examination findings. Different tools generate reports in different formats, such as word processing documents, HTML web pages, and PDF files. Nelson et al. (2008) explained that although these forensic software reports illustrate what, and where evidence is found, it is the examiner's responsibility to explain the significance of the evidence recovered, and define any limitations or un-certainty that applies to the findings.

3.1 Commercial Computer Forensic Tools

Some of the computer forensic tools that generate reports are: FTK, EnCase and Pro-Discover. These tools were examined because of their wide use in digital investiga-tions, and their availability to the authors.

AccessData Forensic Toolkit (FTK version 1.71). The FTK version surveyed in this research was 1.71. FTK contains a full suite of password recovery tools, drive and media wipers, a registry viewer and other useful products. Although FTK .v1.71 comes with its own disk imaging software, it can read the images produced by Encase, Linux DD, SafeBack (up to version 2.0), SMART .s01 and others.

FTK can generate reports in different formats like (.xml, .rtf, .wml, .docx). FTK reports include exported files, custom logos, and external information such as hash lists, search results, and password lists. FTK produces an XML report detailing all the digital evidence items that were bookmarked during the investigation process. A sim-ple XSL style sheet is provided to present this information in a clear and readable manner, and the style sheet can be customized to reflect an investigator's data needs (Nelson et al., 2008).

ProDiscover Forensic Tool (version 5.5). ProDiscover offers forensic examiners an integrated Windows application for the collection, analysis, management, and report-ing of computer disk evidence. ProDiscover version 5.5 forensic edition, supports all

Windows based file systems including FAT 12/16/32 and NTFS Dynamic disks in addition to file systems such as SUN Solaris UFS and Linux Ext 2/3. ProDiscover .v5.5 is completely scriptable using the ProScript interface, and Perl. ProDiscover enables practitioners to locate data on a computer disk while protecting evidence, and creating evidentiary quality reports for use in legal proceedings (ProDiscover, n.d.).

EnCase Forensic Tool (version 6). EnCase is software developed by a company called Guidance Software. It is one of the most common tools used in computer forensics. In this paper, the authors reviewed EnCase version 6. EnCase has an organized user interface that simplifies the viewing of media contents using different views. These views include picture gallery, image evidence, hex, and file tree views. EnCase can also be used to acquire evidence. EnCase provides investigators with a single tool, capable of conducting large-scale investigations from beginning to end (Glendale, 2010).

EnCase has a number of automatically generated reports that can be created. Below are some example reports:

- Listing of all files and folders in a case
- Detailed listing of all URLs and corresponding dates and times that websites were visited
- Document incident report that helps create the required documentation relevant during the incident response process
- Detailed hard drive information about physical and logical partitions

3.2 Standardization

In digital forensics, researchers have described the importance of a standard, open format for digital evidence provenance, both for description and comparison of particular pieces of evidence, as well as for tool interoperability and validation (Levine et al., 2009). Moreover, Pladna (2008) proposed a standard digital evidence bag for a large organization to perform more efficient collection of data. Marcella et al. (2007) explained that a digital forensics laboratory accreditation standard, and standard operating procedure checklists are intended to act as guides to the uniform process of conducting digital forensics examination in a precise and accurate manner. The Common Evidence Format Working Group (2006) proposed defining a standard format for storing and transmitting digital evidence by using metadata so that it can be processed efficiently by multiple tools and parties, can ensure evidence integrity, and effective case management. Garfinkel et al. (2006) designed a file format for a forensic image called the Advanced Forensics Format (AFF). This format is both open and extensible. Like the EnCase format, AFF stores the imaged disk as a series of pages or segments, allowing the image to be compressed for significant savings. Unlike EnCase, AFF allows metadata to be stored either inside the image file or in a separate, companion file. Garfinkel et al. (2006) declared that, although AFF was specifically designed for use in projects involving hundreds or thousands of disk images, it works equally well for practitioners who work with just one or two images. Additionally, if the disk image is corrupted, AFF's internal consistency checks are designed to allow the recovery of as much image data as possible (Garfinkel, et al., 2006).

4 Methodology

In this research, the authors utilized an incremental procedure to develop a standard for reporting digital evidence items in computer forensic tools. There are different types of digital forensics evidence like storage media evidence, memory evidence, network evidence, and mobile device evidence. As a first step, the authors limited their research scope to generated reports for computer forensic evidence items, willing to expand their approach to cover other digital forensics evidence items in their future work.

Primarily, the authors surveyed the reporting function of computer forensic software tools, which were: FTK .v1.71, ProDiscover .v5.5 and Encase .v6 as presented in the literature and software review to formulate the data requirements for digital evidence items. Next, the authors analyzed their findings, and presented them in a tool comparison table. The next step was to conduct a questionnaire targeted at the digital forensics community to verify the data requirement findings for digital evidence items. Finally, based on the findings, and the views of the digital forensics community, the authors defined XML Schema for a proposed XML standard format for reporting digital evidence items in computer forensic tools. This XML standard could be used to facilitate the merger of digital evidence items into a single report by digital forensics practitioners when utilizing multiple computer forensic tools.

5 Discussion and Result

5.1 Computer Forensics Tool Survey

FTK .v1.71, ProDiscover .v5.5 and EnCase .v6 all generate reports related to digital evidence items. Each of these tools include distinct data about digital evidence items in a report. The authors studied reports generated from these tools, and found that these reports contain some common data about digital evidence items. The common data were: File Name, Checksum (e.g. MD5 and SHA1), Created Date, Accessed Date, Modified, Date, File Size, Is Deleted, Comments, Full Path and Extension of the evidence file. Additionally, FTK and EnCase share some data regarding digital evidence items like File Type, Category, Logical Size, Physical Size, Hash Set, and File Offset. On the other hand, ProDiscover has some data about digital evidence items that is not included in FTK and EnCase as demonstrated in Table 1. Some tools cover vast data about digital evidence items like EnCase, and some focus on identifying the cluster, sector, MD5, SHA1, and hidden files like FTK. These differences may suggest a reason behind using different tools in computer forensic examination. Table 1 summarizes the content of the reports generated from ProDiscover, FTK and EnCase.

5.2 Chain of Custody

While surveying the reports generated using computer forensic tools, the authors noticed that the tools did not cover data related to the chain of custody for digital evidence items. Chain of custody is an effective process of documenting the complete journey of the evidence during the life of a case. Rand and Loftus (2003) in their article "Chain of Custody Procedure" declared the chain of custody as a legal term

Table 1. Report data in computer forensic tools

Data	ProDiscover .v5.5	FTK .1.71	EnCase .v6
File Name	✓	✓	✓
Checksum	✓	MD5, SHA1, Hash Set	Hash Value, set, category and properties
Created Date	✓	✓	✓
Accessed Date	✓	✓	✓
Modified Date	✓	✓	✓
File Size	✓	Logical & Physical	Logical, Initialized & Physical
Is Deleted	✓	✓	✓
Comments	✓	✓	✓
STD Info Updated	✓		
MFT Updated	✓		
Bates Num	✓		
Cluster Chain	✓		
Is Preview Available	✓		
Is EXIF Available	✓		
Full Path	Included with file name	✓	✓
Alias		✓	
Extension	Included with file name	✓	✓
File Type		✓	✓
Category		✓	✓
Children		✓	
Descendants		✓	
Encrypted		✓	
Recycled		✓	
Carved		✓	
Indexed		✓	
Sector		✓	
Cluster		✓	
Alternate Name		✓	
Duplicate		✓	✓
Read Only		✓	
System		✓	
Hidden		✓	
Item Number		✓	
Compressed		✓	
KFF		✓	

Table 1. (*continued*)

Bad Extension		✓	
File Offset			✓
Signature			✓
Description			✓
Entry Modified			✓
File Acquired			✓
Initialized Size			✓
Starting Extent			✓
File Extents			✓
Permissions			✓
References			✓
Physical Location			✓
Physical Sector			✓
Evidence File			✓
File Identifier			✓
Code Page			✓
Short Name			✓
Unique Name			✓
Original Path			✓
Symbolic Link			✓
Is Internal			✓
Is Overwritten			✓
Notable			✓
Excluded			✓

that refers to the ability to guarantee the identity, and integrity of the sample (or data) from collection through reporting of the test results. It is a process used to maintain, and document the chronological history of the sample (or data) and the integrity of the evidence (Devine, 2009).

For litigation purposes, regulatory agencies must be able to prove the legal integrity of all samples, and data introduced as evidence (Devine, 2009). Additionally, Rand and Loftus (2003) declared that verification of who has possessed the samples, and where the samples have been is easier if one follows chain-of-custody procedures.

Since there is no way to know in advance which samples, and data may be involved in litigation, the investigator should always follow chain-of-custody procedures whenever samples, and data are collected, transferred, stored, analyzed, or destroyed (Steen & Hassell, 2004). John Petruzzi, director of enterprise security at Constellation Energy explained that, the investigator needs to deal with everything as if it would go to litigation, therefore chain of custody is considered an important process to apply during investigation procedures (Petruzzi, 2005). According to Nelson et al. (2008), an evidence custody form usually contains the following information:

- Case Number
- Investigation Organization
- Investigator
- Nature of Case
- Location evidence was obtained
- Description of evidence
- Evidence recovered by
- Date and time
- Change of custody log (purpose of change, method of transfer, released by, released date, received by, received date, hash value)

At this point, the authors were able to gather the data requirements to define the standard that could be used in reporting digital evidence items in computer forensic tools. However, in order to validate these findings, the authors conducted a questionnaire which is delineated in the section that follows.

5.3 Forensic Community Opinion Questionnaire

To verify the findings regarding the reporting of digital evidence items by computer forensic tools, and the chain of custody, a questionnaire was conducted to acquire the opinion of the stakeholders in the digital forensics community. This questionnaire targeted knowledgeable, and experienced stakeholders in the digital forensics domain. The survey was sent to various lists that contained reputable academics in the area of digital forensics, as well as certified and accredited practitioners. The authors ended up with n=139 responses, of which n=116 were complete.

Respondent demographics. The survey results illustrate that 61% of those who participated were above 40 years old and 29% were between 30 and 40 years old. 91% of the respondents were males. Most of them have higher education degrees, where 61% of those who participated in the study had Bachelor or Diploma degrees, 36% had master degrees and 24% had PhD/doctoral degrees. Regarding the respondents experience in digital forensics, the results indicated that most of the respondents are knowledgeable in the field, where out of 135 responses, 104 respondents had more than five years of experience in the digital forensics field. Additionally, the results showed that most respondents are familiar with using computer forensic software tools, where 135 respondents out of 139 were familiar with computer forensic tools.

The above demographics indicate that the respondents were knowledgeable in the computer forensic domain, and have a reasonably mature level of experience in using computer forensic tools.

Reporting in Computing Forensic Tools. Figure 8 shows the opinion of those respondents regarding reporting in computer forensic tools illustrating the average of the responses. The results can be summarized as follows:

- Reporting function is important in computer forensic tools
- It's common to use more than one computer forensic tool in an investigation
- Reports generated from the tools contain different data structures
- There is a need for a reporting standard in computer forensic tools

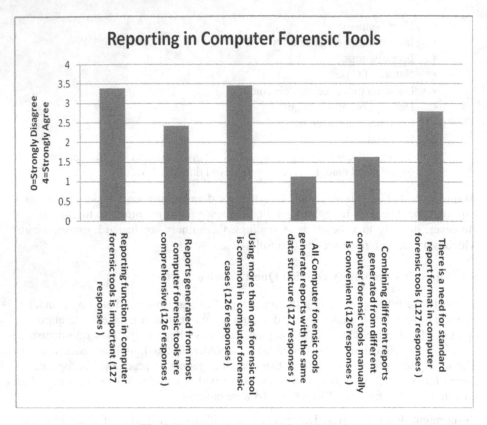

Fig. 3. Reporting in computer forensic tools

Figure 9 illustrates the respondents' opinion regarding the most comprehensive computer forensic tools in reporting evidence items. Out of 123 responses, 45 respondents selected reports combined from multiple tools. Some of those who selected other tools mentioned tools like iLook and X-Ways, and some mentioned that they are using a self-prepared report by adding extracted data from the tools.

Reporting Digital Evidence. The last part in the survey was about the content of the reports, and was divided into four sections, which were: case information, evidence source information, items of interest and chain of custody. The survey questions in this part were created based on the findings in the "Forensic community opinion questionnaire" part of the paper, as well as the literature on the chain of custody for evidence. Figures 10, 11, 12, and 13 show the average results from the responses regarding the data in the reports. The results indicated the surveyed sample's agreement with that data found in the tool-generated reports.

Additionally, some respondents provided the researchers with additional information regarding other data to be included in the computer forensic report. These items are listed below:

-    Time Difference, between the system time and standard local time
-    Systems users

- Operating System and Version
- File System (NTFS, FAT, EXT, etc)
- Encryption deployed
- Write block methods/tools

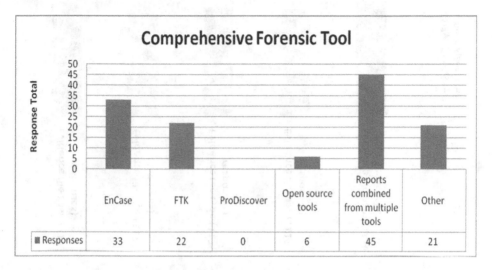

Fig. 4. Comprehensive forensic tool

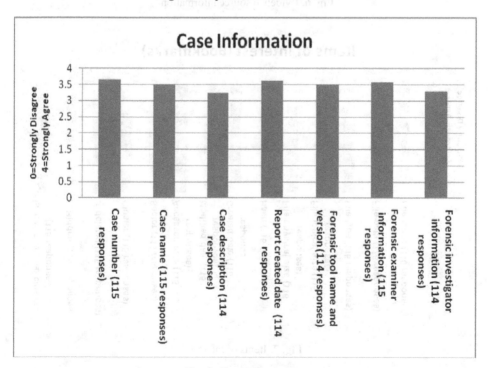

Fig. 5. Case information

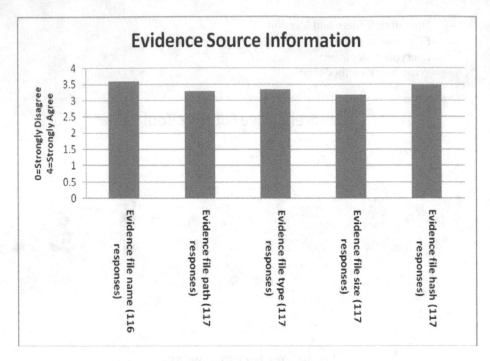

Fig. 6. Evidence source information

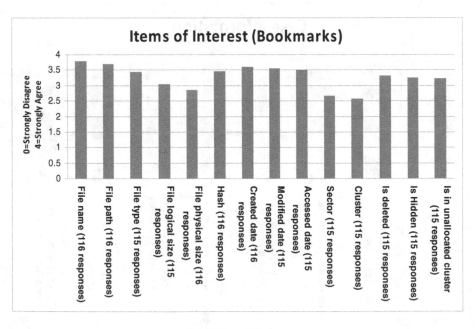

Fig. 7. Items of interest

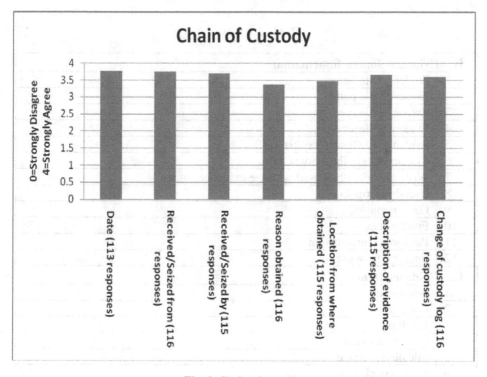

Fig. 8. Chain of custody

- Number and Type of Partitions
- Offset
- Note for each bookmarked item, why the user chose to bookmark it

5.4 Standard Definition

As a result from the previous research findings, the authors identified the data requirements related to digital evidence items. This led the authors to propose the following standard for reporting evidence items in computer forensic tools:

Table 2. Proposed standard for digital evidence item

A.	Case Information
1	Case number
2	Case name
3	Case description
4	Report created date
5	Forensic tool name and version
6	Forensic examiner information (Name, Agency, Address, Phone, Fax, Email, comments)
7	Forensic investigator information (Name, Agency, Address, Phone, Fax, Email, comments)

Table 2. (*continued*)

B.	Evidence Source Information
1	Evidence file name
2	Evidence file path
3	Evidence file type
4	Evidence file size
5	Evidence file hash (checksum)
6	System time in the evidence file
7	Write block method used with the evidence source
8	Users' information
9	OS version
10	File System
11	Partitions' information
12	Encryption in use
C.	**Evidence Item**
1	File name
2	File path
3	File type
4	File logical size
5	File physical size
6	Hash (checksum)
7	Created date
8	Modified date
9	Accessed date
10	Sector
11	Cluster
12	Is deleted
13	Is hidden
14	Is in unallocated cluster
15	Offset
16	Note
D.	**Chain of Custody**
1	Date
2	Received/Seized from
3	Received/Seized by
4	Reason obtained
5	Location from where obtained
6	Description of evidence
7	Change of custody log (purpose of change, method of transfer, released by, released date, received by, received date, hash value)

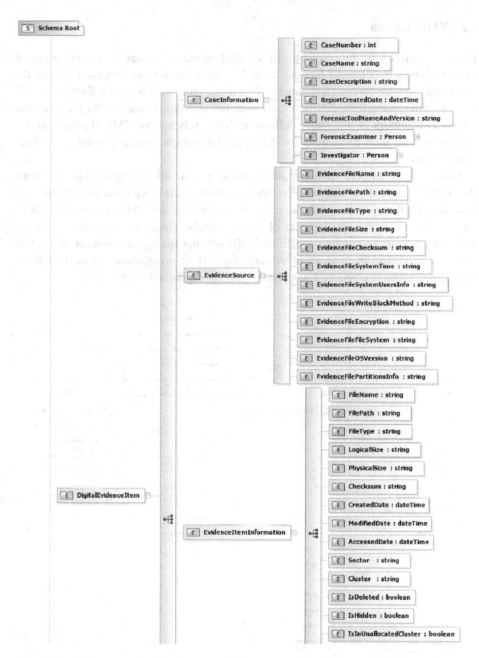

Fig. 9. Visual representation for the proposed data structure for digital evidence item (Part1)

5.5 XML Schema

Here, the authors are proposing to set an XML standard format for reporting digital evidence items in computer forensic tools. Having a standard as such can facilitate the reporting tasks for forensic examiners when using more than one tool. Examiners will end up with reports from different tools with the same data structure for the evidence items. The authors in this paper defined an XML schema for XML standard so this schema can be used to validate the XML digital evidence items generated by computer forensic tools.

Based on the authors' findings, they propose a standard for digital evidence items that includes data about the case, the evidence source, evidence item, and the chain of custody. Additionally, the authors put in their mind that, an XML standard should be flexible to any future development of forensic tools. Therefore, research results enabled the authors in creating a defined XML schema for digital evidence items that can be extended to incorporate other data object if an investigator has to include information, which is consider a new data object for digital evidence items.

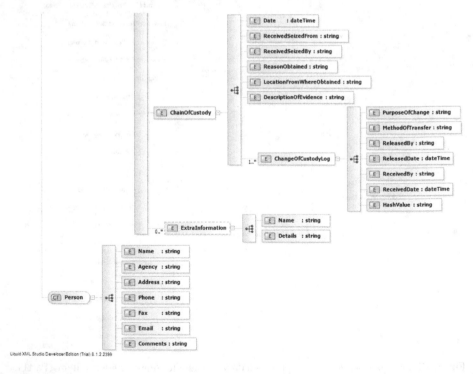

Fig. 10. Visual representation for the proposed data structure for digital evidence item (Part2)

Below is the XML Schema document for the standard defined in Table 2:

```xml
<?xml version="1.0" encoding="UTF-8"?>
<xsd:schema xmlns:tns="http://xml.netbeans.org/schema/forensicReportXmlSchema"
elementFormDefault="qualified"
targetNamespace="http://xml.netbeans.org/schema/forensicReportXmlSchema"
xmlns:xsd="http://www.w3.org/2001/XMLSchema">
    <xsd:element name="DigitalEvidenceItem">
        <xsd:complexType>
            <xsd:sequence>
                <xsd:element name="CaseInformation">
                    <xsd:complexType>
                        <xsd:sequence>
                            <xsd:element name="CaseNumber" type="xsd:int" />
                            <xsd:element name="CaseName" type="xsd:string" />
                            <xsd:element name="CaseDescription" type="xsd:string" />
                            <xsd:element name="ReportCreatedDate" type="xsd:dateTime" />
                            <xsd:element name="ForensicToolNameAndVersion"
type="xsd:string" />
                            <xsd:element name="ForensicExaminer" type="tns:Person" />
                            <xsd:element name="Investigator" type="tns:Person" />
                        </xsd:sequence>
                    </xsd:complexType>
                </xsd:element>
                <xsd:element name="EvidenceSource">
                    <xsd:complexType>
                        <xsd:sequence>
                            <xsd:element name="EvidenceFileName" type="xsd:string" />
                            <xsd:element name="EvidenceFilePath" type="xsd:string" />
                            <xsd:element name="EvidenceFileType" type="xsd:string" />
                            <xsd:element name="EvidenceFileSize" type="xsd:string" />
                            <xsd:element name="EvidenceFileChecksum" type="xsd:string" />
                            <xsd:element name="EvidenceFileSystemTime" type="xsd:string"
/>
                            <xsd:element name="EvidenceFileSystemUsersInfo"
type="xsd:string" />
                            <xsd:element name="EvidenceFileWriteBlockMethod"
type="xsd:string" />
                            <xsd:element name="EvidenceFileEncryption" type="xsd:string"
/>
                            <xsd:element name="EvidenceFileFileSystem" type="xsd:string"
/>
                            <xsd:element name="EvidenceFileOSVersion" type="xsd:string" />
                            <xsd:element name="EvidenceFilePartitionsInfo"
type="xsd:string" />
                        </xsd:sequence>
                    </xsd:complexType>
                </xsd:element>
                <xsd:element name="EvidenceItemInformation">
                    <xsd:complexType>
                        <xsd:sequence>
                            <xsd:element name="FileName" type="xsd:string" />
                            <xsd:element name="FilePath" type="xsd:string" />
                            <xsd:element name="FileType" type="xsd:string" />
                            <xsd:element name="LogicalSize" type="xsd:string" />
                            <xsd:element name="PhysicalSize" type="xsd:string" />
                            <xsd:element name="Checksum" type="xsd:string" />
                            <xsd:element name="CreatedDate" type="xsd:dateTime" />
                            <xsd:element name="ModifiedDate" type="xsd:dateTime" />
                            <xsd:element name="AccessedDate" type="xsd:dateTime" />
                            <xsd:element name="Sector" type="xsd:string" />
                            <xsd:element name="Cluster" type="xsd:string" />
                            <xsd:element name="IsDeleted" type="xsd:boolean" />
                            <xsd:element name="IsHidden" type="xsd:boolean" />
                            <xsd:element name="IsInUnallocatedCluster" type="xsd:boolean"
/>
                            <xsd:element name="Note" type="xsd:string" />
                            <xsd:element name="Offset" type="xsd:string" />
                        </xsd:sequence>
                    </xsd:complexType>
                </xsd:element>
                <xsd:element name="ChainOfCustody">
                    <xsd:complexType>
```

```
                         <xsd:sequence>
                             <xsd:element name="Date" type="xsd:dateTime" />
                             <xsd:element name="ReceivedSeizedFrom" type="xsd:string" />
                             <xsd:element name="ReceivedSeizedBy" type="xsd:string" />
                             <xsd:element name="ReasonObtained" type="xsd:string" />
                             <xsd:element name="LocationFromWhereObtained"
type="xsd:string" />
                             <xsd:element name="DescriptionOfEvidence" type="xsd:string" />
                             <xsd:element name="ChangeOfCustodyLog" maxOccurs="unbounded">
                                 <xsd:complexType>
                                     <xsd:sequence>
                                         <xsd:element name="PurposeOfChange"
type="xsd:string" />
                                         <xsd:element name="MethodOfTransfer"
type="xsd:string" />
                                         <xsd:element name="ReleasedBy" type="xsd:string"
/>
                                         <xsd:element name="ReleasedDate"
type="xsd:dateTime" />
                                         <xsd:element name="ReceivedBy" type="xsd:string"
/>
                                         <xsd:element name="ReceivedDate"
type="xsd:dateTime" />
                                         <xsd:element name="HashValue" type="xsd:string" />
                                     </xsd:sequence>
                                 </xsd:complexType>
                             </xsd:element>
                         </xsd:sequence>
                     </xsd:complexType>
                 </xsd:element>
                 <xsd:element name="ExtraInformation" minOccurs="0" maxOccurs="unbounded">
                     <xsd:complexType>
                         <xsd:sequence>
                             <xsd:element name="Name" type="xsd:string" />
                             <xsd:element name="Details" type="xsd:string" />
                         </xsd:sequence>
                     </xsd:complexType>
                 </xsd:element>
             </xsd:sequence>
         </xsd:complexType>
     </xsd:element>
     <xsd:complexType name="Person">
         <xsd:sequence>
             <xsd:element name="Name" type="xsd:string" />
             <xsd:element name="Agency" type="xsd:string" />
             <xsd:element name="Address" type="xsd:string" />
             <xsd:element name="Phone" type="xsd:string" />
             <xsd:element name="Fax" type="xsd:string" />
             <xsd:element name="Email" type="xsd:string" />
             <xsd:element name="Comments" type="xsd:string" />
         </xsd:sequence>
     </xsd:complexType>
</xsd:schema>
```

6   Conclusion

Presentation of digital evidence is one of the key steps in digital forensics. Reports generated from digital forensics software tools may be used with the official investigation report in order to present digital evidence items to clients, or courts of law. The lack of standards in reporting digital evidence items in digital forensics software tools, leads to difficulties in combining digital evidence items into an official investigation report. This paper proposed a standard data requirement for digital evidence items, that could be used in reports generated using computer forensic tools. The suggested standard covered the basic information about the case, evidence source, items of interest and chain of custody for digital evidence items.

7 Future Work

The authors hope to expand the evaluation of the proposed standard for computer evidence by analyzing open source forensic software tools and their generated reports. Also, the authors are looking forward to implement a tool to manipulate the proposed standard for digital evidence. This tool will allow digital forensics stakeholders to import XML documents generated using different computer forensic tools, and combine them into a central repository, that could generate a standard report to be added to the final investigative report. Another future vision the authors are looking for, is to develop a standard format that goes beyond computer forensic evidence items, and covers other types of digital forensics evidence items like memory forensics, network forensics, and small scale digital device digital evidence items.

References

1. The Common Evidence Format Working Group (Carrier, B., Casey, E, Garfinkel, S., Kornblum, J., Hosmer, C., Rogers, M., Turner, P.): Standardizing Digital Evidence Storage. Communications of the ACM (February 2006)
2. Anson, S., Bunting, S.: Mastering Windows Network Forensics and Investigation. Wiley Publishing, Inc., Canada (2007)
3. Devine, J.: The Importance of the Chain of Custody (October 30, 2009), http://ezinearticles.com/?The-Importance-of-the-Chain-of-Custody&id=3182472 (retrieved March 18, 2010)
4. Garfinkel, S., Malan, S., Dubec, K., Stevens, C., Pham, C.: Disk Imaging with the Advanced Forensics Format, Library and Tools. In: The Second Annual IFIP WG 11.9 International Conference on Digital Forensics, National Center for Forensic Science, Orlando, Florida, USA, January 29-February 1 (2006)
5. Glendale, D.: Guidance Software EnCase (2010), retrieved from http://www.digitalintelligence.com/software/guidancesoftware/encase/
6. Levine, B., Liberatore, M.: DEX: Digital evidence provenance supporting reproducibility and comparison. Digital Investigation 6, S48–S56 (2009)
7. Liquid Technologies Limited: Liquid XML Studio 2010 (version 8.1.2.2399), [Software] available from http://www.liquid-technologies.com/
8. Marcella, A.J., Menendez Jr., D.: Cyber Forensics: A Field Manual for Collecting, Examining, and Preserving Evidence of Computer Crimes. In: Information Security, 2nd edn. Auerbach publications, Taylor & Francis Group (2007)
9. Nelson, B., Phillips, A., Enfringer, F., Steuart, C.: Guide to Computer Forensics and Investigations. GEX Publishing Services, Canada (2008)
10. Petruzzi, J.: How to Keep a Digital Chain of Custody (December 01, 2005), retrieved from http://www.csoonline.com/article/220718/How_to_Keep_a_Digital_Chain_of_Custody
11. Pladna, B.: Computer Forensics Procedures, Tools, and Digital Evidence Bags: What They Are and Who Should Use Them. East Carolina University, East Carolina (2008)
12. ProDiscover. (n.d.) Technology Pathways, http://www.techpathways.com/DesktopDefault.aspx?tabindex=3&tabid=12 (retrieved February 22, 2010)
13. Rand, A., Loftus, T.: Chain of Custody Procedure (2003), retrieved from http://www.lagoonsonline.com/laboratory-articles/custody.htm
14. Steen, S., Hassell, J.: Computer Forensics 101 (October 2004), retrieved from http://www.expertlaw.com/library/forensic_evidence/computer_forensics_101.html

Signature Based Detection of User Events for Post-mortem Forensic Analysis

Joshua Isaac James[*,**], Pavel Gladyshev, and Yuandong Zhu

Centre for Cybercrime Investigation
University College Dublin
Belfield, Dublin 4, Ireland
{Joshua.James,Pavel.Gladyshev,Yuandong.Zhu}@UCD.ie

Abstract. This paper introduces a novel approach to user event reconstruction by showing the practicality of generating and implementing signature-based analysis methods to reconstruct high-level user actions from a collection of low-level traces found during a post-mortem forensic analysis of a system. Traditional forensic analysis and the inferences an investigator normally makes when given digital evidence, are examined. It is then demonstrated that this natural process of inferring high-level events from low-level traces may be encoded using signature-matching techniques. Simple signatures using the defined method are created and applied for three popular Windows-based programs as a proof of concept.

Keywords: Digital Forensics, Event Reconstruction, Signature Detection, User Actions, User Events, Investigator inference.

1 Introduction

The method of using signatures to detect certain types of actions or events is commonplace in many information security related products such as Antivirus and Intrusion Detection Systems (IDS)[12][13]. In these systems, signature based methods have proven to be effective when a known pattern can be tested for. These patterns can range from malicious code embedded in a file, to detecting port scans within a network. "Signatures offer unparalleled percision in detection and forensics... This gives you a clear understanding of exactly what attacks took place... [also] since signatures look for very specific events, they generate a much lower false positive rate..." [6]. The downside, however, is that "traditional signature-based antivirus and antispyware fail to detect zero-day exploits or targeted, custom-tailored attacks" [10], which is a huge disadvantage against todays highly dynamic malware.

Some detection methods have been proposed [5][7] that attempt to model user activities. These methods use data-mining techniques to extract signatures of user activities that may then be tested for. However, these methods examine network traffic from a controlled environment where logging is possible, rather than sparse

---

[*] Research funded by the Science Foundation Ireland (SFI) under Research Frontiers Programme 2007 grant CMSF575.
[**] This Research was conducted using equipment funded by the Higher Education Authority of Ireland under the Research Equipment Renewal Grant Scheme.

I. Baggili (Ed.): ICDF2C 2010, LNICST 53, pp. 96–109, 2011.

after-the-fact event information in an uncontrolled environment like an investigator may encounter.

File-system signature analysis (much like an antivirus) has also previously been proposed [2] in an attempt to automate the identification of suspect media files on storage media. While this method does use signature-based file-system analysis, it focuses on the signature of a type of file and is uninterested in the action that *caused* the file.

The previously described methods endeavor to detect malicious eventsmostly with large amounts of real-time (or logged) data. [2] uses signatures to detect malicious files on a system, but so much more that simple file detection is possible using signature-based analysis. This paper applies signature-based detection in a novel way. The focus is on signatures of user behaviors, where the signature of a *user action* is defined. These signatures are used *after* the incident to detect user actions that have taken place, unlike traditional methods that are used as prevention systems. These signatures are also applied at a system-wide level, looking at the state of the system as a whole, rather than focusing on a single file that may be associated with an activity.

1.1 Contribution

This paper introduces a novel approach to user event reconstruction by showing the practicality of generating and implementing signature-based analysis methods to reconstruct high-level user actions from a collection of low-level traces found during a post-mortem forensic analysis of a system. Specific signatures for common user Windows-based actions are applied as a proof-of-concept for signature-based forensic analysis.

1.2 Organization

This paper begins with an overview of traditional analysis of evidence found within a suspect system. Traditional traces used in an investigation and the inference process that investigators use and the current state of signature-based detection of user events will be discussed. After which, a short background of Windows timestamps will be given. Section three then demonstrates the proposed method used to derive evidential traces that comprise the basis for the signatures of user actions. Update categories of timestamps are defined which are later used in the creation of these signatures. The signature creation and application process is then shown using Internet Explorer 8 as an example. A demonstration of the application of created signatures is then given using generated signatures for two additional commonly used Windows-based programs. Finally, the results and future of such a technique are considered.

2   Traditional Analysis in an Investigation

In traditional digital investigations timestamp information is often used in the analysis phase. Timestamps associated with logs, files, and even registry entries give investigators clues about when certain events took place. However, "use of timestamps as evidence can be questionable due to the reference to a clock with unknown adjustment" [14]. Several methods [9][16][14] to verify the consistency and validity of this valuable timestamp information have been suggested. Other information, such as inferred event times relative to known events [1][16], can also be derived from traces on a system.

As described in [4][15] the Windows Registry contains much information about user activities. Some, such as Most Recently Used (MRU) lists, contain information that can be directly extracted, while other information, such as the meaning of the order of MRU items through time, must be inferred. Investigators observe these traces of evidence on a system and naturally make inferences as to their meanings based on their knowledge of the system and past experiences. The method proposed in this paper attempts to incorporate both extracted and inferred information to automate more of the observed and inferred user event analysis an investigator would normally do during an investigation, with less error and inferential bias.

2.1 Automatic Detection of User Events

When analyzing evidence, investigators normally gather information in two ways: by direct observation and by the inference of one fact from the observation of others. Human inference, however, is prone to assumption and error [8]. To accurately infer information from given facts an investigator must understand the underlying relation between the observed facts and the inferred conclusion. For example Zhu [17] states, "To infer events from the Registry it requires an investigator to understand the relationship between Registry information and occurred activities". This means that when a user does an action that affects data stored in the Windows Registry, the investigator can only begin to infer what the user action was once the investigator understands not only *how* but also *why* that particular piece of data has been modified in the registry.

This paper proposes the theory that both the direct observation and inference phases of an investigation of user actions can be automated using signature-based detection methods. By determining the user activity traces that normally appear in a system after a user event, it is possible to automatically 'infer' the occurrence of the event based on the observable traces. In this paper the focus will be limited to time-stamps associated with the files and registry entries. Other traces, such as file fragments in slack space, could also denote user actions, but the scope of this paper is intentionally limited to provide a simple proof of concept. A signature will be defined as a collection of timestamps modified by the occurrence of the event. The hypothesis is that when an event occurs the associated timestamps are updated within a short period of time. As a result, the occurrence of the event may be inferred by observing that the corresponding ensemble of timestamps have been updated within short time of each other. The experiment described in the following sections has been conducted to verify this theory.

2.2 Windows Timestamps

The availability of timestamps differs between different versions of Microsoft Windows. The 'Last Access Time' has been disabled by default for performance reasons in Visa, 2008 and Windows 7. However, "disabling last access update does not mean that the Accessed Date on files does not get updated *at all*; it means that it does not get updated on directory listing or file opening, but last accessed can sometimes be updated when a file is modified and is updated when a file is moved between volumes" [9]. Pre-Vista versions of Windows using the NTFS file system, including Windows 2003, do have last accessed timestamps enabled by default. In all Windows versions, modified and created timestamps are unable to be disabled. Likewise, the

Windows Registry provides "[Key Cells] that contain the timestamp of the most recent update to the [Registry] key" [11]. These keys' timestamps can also not be disabled, providing a valuable resource to investigators.

3 Deriving User Action Signatures for Internet Explorer

In this section we will discuss the process of deriving signatures for a given user action, in this case "opening Internet Explorer", and show how these signatures can be practically applied. User actions and the concept of causality have previously been discussed in [17]. The same definition of user actions applies, where a user action is an interaction between the user and the system, but in this paper the definition will be applied to the entire system and not only the Windows Registry. The experiment in this section will be conducted on a Windows XP SP3 computer with Internet Explorer 8.0.6001.18702, all with default settings. Windows XP was chosen because according to [3] it is still the most commonly encountered operating system in digital investigations. The first step to defining a signature that can be used to detect a certain user action is to determine the traces that are uniquely updated because of that particular user action.

3.1 Determining Traces for the Signature

Microsoft Process Monitor[1] (procmon) was used to record all system calls executed during the user action "opening Internet Explorer 8 (IE8)". The initial tests recorded all system activity. In order to remove noise (unrelated system calls) generated by other running processes, IE8 was started while recording. This action was executed 400 times per test, after which the entries that were not present during every run were removed. Three of these tests were conducted. The filtering process reduced the number of traces from around 11,000 to approximately 4,000 (Fig. 1), however consistent noise was still found to be present.

Using this data it was determined that by filtering the Process Monitor output with the selected program's process name (iexplore.exe), as well as the "explorer.exe" process, similar results of around 4,000 traces could be achieved without needing to repeat the action multiple times.

To determine the traces associated with starting IE8, Process Monitor was started and configured to filter out events not associated with the "iexplore.exe" and "explorer.exe" processes. The procmon capture was then cleared and IE8 was opened. The procmon capture was stopped and exported as a comma separated value (.csv) file. Unique file and registry entries were filtered to a file named "traces.sig". The resulting file contains a list of the names and paths of files and registry keys that are accessed during the opening of Internet Explorer 8. It contained 3,915 file and registry traces. Most of which, however, were registry entries that were not Registry keys and therefore have no associated timestamp information. From this list a total of 156 files and 611 registry keys with associated timestamp information were found. A Perl script 'sigtest.pl' was written to retrieve the associated file and registry timestamp information from the items in this list.

---

[1] http://technet.microsoft.com/en-us/sysinternals/bb896645.aspx

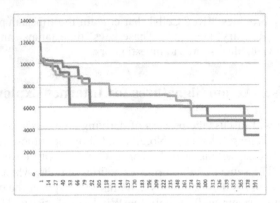

Fig. 1. Removal of noise caused by background processes where the x-axis is the number of times IE8 has been run and the y-axis is the number of traces common to each test

To observe the pattern in which the identified trace's timestamps are updated when the user action takes place, Internet Explorer 8 was opened as before. The difference from the first phase is that procmon was not used, and after each opening of IE8, 'sigtest.pl' was executed to output the timestamps of the file and registry entries in the previously created 'traces.sig' file. This process was carried out 10 times over three days. From the produced data, timestamps of the traces can be categorized to determine important event traces as well as update patterns of the final signature.

3.2 Analysis of Timestamp Updates

From the data produced in section 7.1, 122 file and registry traces were identified as relevant to the tested user action. This section will list the observed update patterns that will be used to define specific timestamp update categories. Note that, in Windows XP, each file has three associated timestamps, and therefore may count multiple times.

- *Always Updated File and Registry Key Timestamps (AU)*: It was observed that 21 file and registry timestamps were updated each time IE8 was opened. Of these, 9 files had updated 'accessed' times, 10 files had updated 'modified' times, and 9 registry keys had updated 'modified' times. These timestamps can be further subdivided into five update categories based on the uniqueness of their observed update patterns. These subcategories are explained as follows and are summarized in (Table 1):

Table 1. IE8 *Always Updated* Sub-Category Update Patterns

	Modified Time	Accessed Time	Created Time
AU1	Updated	Updated	Unchanged
AU2	Updated	Updated	Inconsistent
AU3	Unchanged	Updated	Unchanged
AU4	N/A	Updated	N/A
AU5	Updated	Unchanged	Unchanged

- o *AU1*: Three files from this group were found to update their accessed and modified timestamps every time Internet Explorer was started, but also with the execution of unrelated actions. Of these files it can be said that their updated timestamps must be greater-than or equal to the time of the most recent execution of IE8. It was also observed that the created timestamps of these files is less-than or equal to the installation of the system itself.
- o *AU2*: Three files were observed to have their accessed and modified timestamps updated with each execution of IE8. Of these files, one was the prefetch[2] file for Internet Explorer. Its created timestamp was found to correlate with the first time Internet Explorer was run on the system. Only the accessed and modified times were updated with each user action. The other two files were Internet Explorer 'cookie' files correlating to 'administrator@live[1].txt' and 'administrator@msn[1].txt' where 'administrator' is the name of the local user account. The accessed and modified timestamps of these files were updated with each user action, and the created timestamps were found to update often with the user action, but not always and with no discernable pattern. Of these files it can be said that any timestamp happening before the most recent user event denotes the time of a previous user event.
- o *AU3*: Four files were found to have only their modified, and not their accessed, times updated with each opening of Internet Explorer 8.
- o *AU4*: Nine Registry keys were identified that always had their associated timestamp information updated.
- o *AU5*: Two files were found to have only it's accessed timestamps updated: IExplore.exe and shell32.dll.

- • *Timestamps Updated on the First Run Only (FRO)*: It was observed that 1 registry timestamp was updated only during the first opening of IE8 per session.
- • *Usage-Based File Timestamp Updates (UB)*: It was observed that 4 Windows shortcut (.lnk) files' accessed timestamps were updated often, but not always when they were used to start IE8. If they were not used to start IE8 they were never updated by the action.
- • *Irregular Update of Timestamps (IU)*: It was observed that 93 files had irregular timestamp update patterns, and each in this category had only its accessed timestamp updated.

- o *IU1*: Although the majority of the traces categorized as IU are seemingly irregular, it was observed that cookies within the user's "\Cookies" folder were updated on the first run of the session, and then irregularly updated during the starting of IE8 in the same user session, making cookie files a combination of *FRO* and *IU*.

---

[2] More information about prefetch files can be found at:
`http://www.microsoft.com/whdc/archive/XP_kernel.mspx#ECLAC`

3.3   Categories of Timestamps

From the observed update patterns, four primary categories of timestamp updates can be defined. Two important observations apply to each category. First, trace updates are *caused* by a user action, such as double-clicking an icon causes a program to execute. This process is not instantaneous and therefore any observable traces were created or updated some time *after* the actual user action. Second, it was observed that each trace was updated within one minute of the user action. This means that the update process must also be defined as a *time-span* and is not instantaneous.

Category 1: *Always Updated Timestamps* – 6 files and registry entries with timestamp information were consistently updated each time, and only when, Internet Explorer 8 was opened.Traces that are always updated by opening IE8, as well as by other user actions, have been removed. The remaining traces in this category will provide the core of the signature, as they are the most reliably updated.

```
Always Updated ( TS >= Run Time )
C:\WINDOWS\Prefetch\IEXPLORE.EXE-27122324.pf
C:\Documents and Settings\Administrator\Local Settings\Application Data\Microsoft\Feeds Cache\index.dat
HKEY_CURRENT_USER\Software\Microsoft\CTF\TIP
HKEY_CURRENT_USER\Software\Microsoft\Internet Explorer\Security\AntiPhishing\2CEDBFBC-DBA8-43AA-B1FD-CC8E6316E3E2
HKEY_CURRENT_USER\Software\Microsoft\Windows\CurrentVersion\Ext\Stats\{E2E2DD38-D088-4134-82B7-F2BA38496583}\iexplore
HKEY_CURRENT_USER\Software\Microsoft\Windows\CurrentVersion\Ext\Stats\{FB5F1910-F110-11D2-BB9E-00C04F795683}\iexplore
```

Fig. 2. IE8 file and registry traces updated each time IE8 is opened

Category 2: *Timestamps Updated on theFirst Run Only* – One registry entry and all cookie files were found to have their timestamp information consistently updated on the first run of Internet Explorer 8 *per user session* (Fig. 3).

```
First Run of Session (Supporting, Past Run Times)
HKEY_CURRENT_USER\Software\Microsoft\Windows\CurrentVersion\Explorer\MenuOrder\Favorites\Links
```

Fig. 3. IE8 registry trace updated during the first run of the session

Category 3: *Irregular Update of Timestamps* – 93 files were found to have their timestamps updated in an irregular fashion (Appendix A).

Category 4: *Usage-Based Timestamp Update* – 4 Windows shortcut files were identified that were inconsistently updated when the particular link file itself was used (Fig. 4), and never during the starting of IE8 when the file itself was not used.

```
Usage-Based Update (not updated every use, Supporting, Past Run Times)
C:\Documents and Settings\Administrator\Desktop\Internet Explorer.lnk
C:\Documents and Settings\Administrator\Start Menu\Programs\Inernet Explorer.lnk
C:\Documents and Settings\Administrator\Application Dat'\Microsoft\Internet Explorer\Quick Launch\Launch Internet Explorer Browser.lnk
C:\Documents and Settings\Administrator\Start Menu\Programs\Accessories\System Tools\Internet Explorer (No Add-ons).lnk
```

Fig. 4. IE8 file traces updated on file usage (link files)

Also from the original traces list there were a number of file and registry entries that were never updated during the opening of IE8. These entries have been discarded.

By using the different categories of timestamps previously explained, signatures that match the known timestamp update patterns can now be derived.

3.4 Signature Generalization

Once a list of traces associated with a certain user action is generated and classified, the traces must then be generalized to be portable. To do this, any user or system-specific paths would have to be generalized. Taking the Category 1 Windows prefetch file as an example:

C:\Windows\Prefetch\IEXPLORE.EXE-27122324.pf

The system-unique identifiers would need to be replaced with variables, as so:

%SystemRoot%\Prefetch\IEXPLORE.EXE-**%s**.pf

Where the variable %SystemRoot% is the location of the Windows system folder including the drive and path, and %s is a string of numbers and letters.

The generalization should include the possibility that programs may be installed in non-default locations. This means that other information sources, such as reading the installation path from the Windows Registry[3], would be required. This generalization will allow signatures generated on one system to be used in the analysis of other computers. While generalizing signatures with simple variables (as above) can be automated, determining the best method for generalizing signatures while still ensuring the detection of the correct objects is currently being explored.

3.5 Creation of the Signature for Opening Internet Explorer

A signature in the context of this paper is defined as a collection of timestamps modified by the occurrence of an event. By using the previously defined categories of timestamps as well as the observations of update patterns within these categories, a signature of a particular user action can be created by defining the pattern in which associated trace timestamps are updated during the occurrence of the user action.

Category 1 traces will provide the Core of the created signatures. The reason for this is that the modified timestamps in this group must always be updated given a user opening IE8. Due to theinconsistent nature of the other category types, they will be defined as 'supporting evidence'. Supporting evidence can enhance the probability, or believability, of a detected user action, but the issue of probability is beyond the scope of this paper.

Based on observations relating to the always-updated file and registry key timestamps (timestamp Category 1), a signature can be defined. Using traces that are always updated *only* by opening IE8,the execution of the user action can be inferred from these traces if all the traces display consistent update information. In this case consistency means that each trace has a timestamp that has been updated within 1 minute of each other. If the traces are not consistent with each other, then nothing can be inferred since some unknown, uncommon action must have updated the traces in an unexpected way. Consider the Core traces from IE8 (generalized):

---

[3] One Windows Registry key containing installed program path information is:
  HKEY_LOCAL_MACHINE\Software\Microsoft\Windows\CurrentVersion\Uninstall

- %SystemRoot%\Prefetch\IEXPLORE.EXE-%s.pf
- %HomeDrive%\%HomePath%\Local Settings\Application
  Data\Microsoft\Feeds Cache\index.dat
- HKEY_USERS\%SID\Software\Microsoft\CTF\TIP
- HKEY_USERS\%SID\Software\Microsoft\Internet
  Explorer\Security\AntiPhishing\%s
- HKEY_USERS\%SID\Software\Microsoft\Windows\CurrentVersion\Ext\St
  ats\{%s}\iexplore

These traces are updated every time, and only, when the user action "open Internet Explorer 8" is executed. The collection of modified timestamps of the detected traces may then be tested for consistency: whether each timestamp has been updated within 1 minute of each other. This process is shown below.

For the first test IE8 was executed on a Windows XP system at 2:30pm on the 12th of April 2010. Various other programs such as Mozilla Firefox, Windows Live Messenger, Outlook Express, and others were used to browse the Internet, chat and check email, respectively. These actions took place over two days without another execution of IE8. During the evenings the computer was shut down, and was restarted the next morning. The following table (Table 2) shows the timestamps of the IE8 traces analyzed on the 14th of April 2010.

Table 2. "Open IE8" Signature Analysis conducted at 4:45pm 14/4/2010

Trace Name	Timestamp
C:\WINDOWS\Prefetch\IEXPLORE.EXE-27122324.pf	4/12/2010 14:30:37
C:\Documents and Settings\Administrator\Local Settings\Application Data\Microsoft\Feeds Cache\index.dat	4/12/2010 14:30:26
HKEY_USERS\S-1-5-21-1417001333-573735546-682003330-500\Software\Microsoft\CTF\TIP	4/12/2010 2:30 PM
HKEY_USERS\S-1-5-21-1417001333-573735546-682003330-500\Software\Microsoft\Internet Explorer\Security\AntiPhishing\2CEDBFBC-DBA8-43AA-B1FD-CC8E6316E3E2	4/12/2010 2:30 PM
HKEY_USERS\S-1-5-21-1417001333-573735546-682003330-500\Software\Microsoft\Windows\CurrentVersion\Ext\Stats\{E2E2DD38-D088-4134-82B7-F2BA38496583}\iexplore	4/12/2010 2:30 PM
HKEY_USERS\S-1-5-21-1417001333-573735546-682003330-500\Software\Microsoft\Windows\CurrentVersion\Ext\Stats\{FB5F1910-F110-11D2-BB9E-00C04F795683}\iexplore	4/12/2010 2:30 PM

Each trace has a timestamp that was updated within 1 minute of 2:30pm, and all correlate to the time Internet Explorer was last opened. Next IE8 was opened again on the 14th of April 2010 at 5:00pm. The trace timestamps were analyzed at 5:19pm, the result of which is shown in table 3.

Each trace has a timestamp that was updated within 1 minute of 5:00pm, and all correlate to the time Internet Explorer was last opened.

Table 3. "Open IE8" Signature Analysis conducted at 5:19pm 14/4/2010

Trace Name	Timestamp
C:\WINDOWS\Prefetch\IEXPLORE.EXE-27122324.pf	4/14/2010 17:00:24
C:\Documents and Settings\Administrator\Local Settings\Application Data\Microsoft\Feeds Cache\index.dat	4/14/2010 17:00:19
HKEY_USERS\S-1-5-21-1417001333-573735546-682003330-500\Software\Microsoft\CTF\TIP	4/14/2010 5:00 PM
HKEY_USERS\S-1-5-21-1417001333-573735546-682003330-500\Software\Microsoft\Internet Explorer\Security\AntiPhishing\2CEDBFBC-DBA8-43AA-B1FD-CC8E6316E3E2	4/14/2010 5:00 PM
HKEY_USERS\S-1-5-21-1417001333-573735546-682003330-500\Software\Microsoft\Windows\CurrentVersion\Ext\Stats\{E2E2DD 38-D088-4134-82B7-F2BA38496583}\iexplore	4/14/2010 5:00 PM
HKEY_USERS\S-1-5-21-1417001333-573735546-682003330-500\Software\Microsoft\Windows\CurrentVersion\Ext\Stats\{FB5F191 0-F110-11D2-BB9E-00C04F795683}\iexplore	4/14/2010 5:00 PM

Since these timestamps must be updated when the user action takes place, and the updates are caused only by the user action, then if all these timestamps are consistent then it can be inferred that the user action that caused the updates took place shortly before the detected timestamps.

3.6 Further Application of Signatures

To determine whether this approach is applicable to programs other than IE8, signatures of user actions for Firefox 3.6 and MSN Messenger 2009 were created using the process described earlier.

3.6.1 Detecting the Opening of Firefox 3.6
For Firefox 3.6 (FF3.6) the user action of "opening Firefox 3.6" was tested. 1,507 original traces were updated when FF3.6 was opened. Of these, only 1 file was determined to have always updated (Category 1) timestamps. This file was the standard Windows pre-fetch file:

C:\WINDOWS\Prefetch\FIREFOX.EXE-28641590.pf

Other traces were identified as being updated when FF3.6 was opened, but were also updated when FF3.6 was used to browse the Internet or when the program was closed. Because only one trace is available other sources of user event information will need to be identified to ensure this trace is consistent with the system, thereby increasing the reliability of the observed and inferred information.

3.6.2 Detecting the Opening of MSN Messenger 2009
For MSN Messenger 2009 (MSN2009) the user action of "opening MSN Messenger 2009" was tested. 4,263 original traces were updated when MSN2009 was opened. Of these, 3 unique traces were determined to have always updated (Category 1) timestamps.

- %HomeDrive%\%HomePath%\Tracing\WindowsLiveMessenger-uccapi-%i.uccapilog
- %SystemRoot%\Prefetch\MSNMSGR.EXE-%s.pf
- HKEY_USERS\%SID\Software\Microsoft\Tracing\WPPMedia

To test this signature MSN2009 was started at 7:28pm on the 14th of April 2010. At 7:29pm MSN2009 was closed. IE8, FF3.6 and Outlook Express were then used to surf the Internet and check email. The signature analysis was then conducted at 7:49pm on the same day. The results of the analysis are shown in table 4.

Table 4. "Open MSN2009" Signature Analysis conducted at 7:49pm 14/4/2010

Trace Name	Timestamp
C:\Documents and Settings\Administrator\Tracing\WindowsLiveMessenger-uccapi-0.uccapilog	4/14/2010 19:28:25
C:\WINDOWS\Prefetch\MSNMSGR.EXE-030AB647.pf	4/14/2010 19:28:25
HKEY_USERS\S-1-5-21-1417001333-573735546-682003330-500\Software\Microsoft\Tracing\WPPMedia	4/14/2010 7:28 PM

Each trace has a timestamp that was updated within 1 minute of 7:28pm, and all correlate to the time MSN2009 was last opened. Next MSN2009 was opened again on the 14th of April 2010 at 7:56pm. The trace timestamps were analyzed at 7:58pm, the result of which is shown in table 5.

Table 5. "Open MSN2009" Signature Analysis conducted at 7:58pm 14/4/2010

Trace Name	Timestamp
C:\Documents and Settings\Administrator\Tracing\WindowsLiveMessenger-uccapi-0.uccapilog	4/14/2010 19:56:46
C:\WINDOWS\Prefetch\MSNMSGR.EXE-030AB647.pf	4/14/2010 19:56:46
HKEY_USERS\S-1-5-21-1417001333-573735546-682003330-500\Software\Microsoft\Tracing\WPPMedia	4/14/2010 7:56 PM

Each trace has a timestamp that was updated within 1 minute of 7:56pm, and all correlate to the time MSN2009 was last opened. It can be inferred that the user action "open MSN2009" must have taken place shortly before the detected timestamps.

4 Conclusions

Traditional analysis in a digital investigation is currently a highly manual process. With the growing amount of data an investigator must analyze, automated analysis techniques are necessary. This paper demonstrated how signature-based detection methods could be used to detect defined user actions by inferring information from the patterns in which traces are updated for the given user action. A simple signature for a particular user action has been created and applied to automatically detect the last occurrence of a user action during a post-mortem investigation. Even though detection of simple user actions for three programs has been shown, this technique does not fully utilize all the observable information, requires much more extensive testing across many systems, and has yet to demonstrate its practicality for the detection of more complex user actions. For these reasons there is still much work to be done.

4.1 Limitations

The current limitation of this technique appears to be the signature itself. The complexity of the signature generation, and the varying traces generated between different versions of the same software will make maintenance prohibitive. It is because of this that both specific and general signature types need to be explored. With multiple signature types general signatures may detect any type of a certain action (such as any software installation action) and specific signatures will be used for actions that are specifically important to an investigator.

4.2 Future Work

Based on the results obtained in this paper it appears that signature-based detection of user actions is possible, however much work needs to be done. Requirements include making the signatures portable, specifically looking at programs installed in non-default locations. Others include improving the usage of information gained from observable traces, i.e. what other information can be inferred. This area includes the introduction of probability by attempting to capitalize on the 'supporting evidence' defined earlier. Also the detection of 'exact matches' within the Core signature may prove to provide supporting information that may help ensure the consistency and integrity of the observed, and thus inferred, information. The detection of not only the most recent time a user action has happened, but also previous executions of the user action based on the observable information and the profiling of user behavior are also under consideration.

References

1. Gladyshev, P., Patel, A.: Formalising Event Time Bounding in Digital Investigations. International Journal of Digital Evidence 4 (2005)
2. Haggerty, J., Taylor, M.: FORSIGS: Forensic Signature Analysis of the Hard Drive for Multimedia File Fingerprints. In: IFIP International Federation for Information Processing, vol. 232, pp. 1–12 (2007)
3. James, J.: Survey of Evidence and Forensic Tool Usage in Digital Investigations (July 23, 2010), The UCD Centre for Cybercrime Investigation, http://cci.ucd.ie/content/survey-evidence-and-forensic-tool-usage-digital-investigations (July 26, 2010)
4. Kahvedzic, D., Kechadi, T.: Extraction of user activity through comparison of windows restore points. In: 6th Australian Digital Forensics Conference (2008)
5. Kim, D.H., In, D.H.: Cyber Criminal Activity Analysis Models using Markov Chain for Digital Forensics. In: ISA, pp. 193–198 (2008)

6. McAfee. Complete Security: The Case for Combined Behavioral and Signature-Based Protection. Whitepaper. Santa Carla: McAfee Inc. (2005)
7. Mukkamala, S., Sung, A.H.: Identifying Significant Features for Network Forensic Analysis Using Artificial Intelligent Techniques. International Journal of Digital Evidence 1.4 (2003)
8. Ogawa, A., Yamazaki, Y., Ueno, K., Cheng, K., Iriki, A.: Neural Correlates of Species-typical Illogical Cognitive Bias in Human Inference. Journal of Cognitive Neuroscience, Massachusetts Institute of Technology (2009), doi:10.1162/jocn.2009.21330
9. Personage, H.: The Meaning of (L)inkfiles (I)n (F)orensic (E)xaminations (November 2009). Computer Forensics Miscellany, http://computerforensics.parsonage.co.uk/downloads/TheMeaningofLIFE.pdf (Febuary 2, 2010)
10. Roiter, N.: When signature based antivirus isn't enough (May 3, 2007), http://searchsecurity.techtarget.com/news/article/0,289142,sid14_gci1253602,00.html (Febuary 2, 2010)
11. Russinovich, M.: Inside the Registry (Feburary 3, 2010), http://technet.microsoft.com/enus/library/cc750583.aspx
12. Scarfone, K., Mell, P.: Guide to Intrusion Detection and Prevention Systems (IDPS) SP800-94. Special Publication. NIST: National Institute of Science and Technology. National Institute of Science and Technology, Gaithersburg (2007)
13. Sy, B.K.: Signature-Based Approach for Intrusion Detection. Machine Learning and Data Mining in Pattern Recognition, 526–536 (August 8, 2005)
14. Willassen, S.Y.: Timestamp evidence correlation by model based clock hypothesis testing. In: Proceedings of the 1st International Conference on Forensic Applications and Techniques in Telecommunications, Information, and Multimedia and Workshop, ICST, Brussels, Belgium, pp. 1–6 (2008)
15. Zhu, Y., James, J., Gladyshev, P.: A comparative methodology for the reconstruction of digital events using Windows Restore Points. Digital Investigation (2009a), doi:10.1016/j.diin.2009.02.004
16. Zhu, Y., James, J., Gladyshev, P.: Consistency Study of the Windows Registry. In: Sixth Annual IFIP WG 11.9 International Conference on Digital Forensics (2010)
17. Zhu, Y., Gladyshev, P., James, J.: Using ShellBag Information to Reconstruct User Activities. Digital Investigation 6, 69–77 (2009c), doi:10.1016/j.diin.2009.06.009

Appendix

Appendix A: List of Category 3 Traces for Internet Explorer– Irregularly Updated.

C:\Documents and Settings\Administrator\Cookies*,
C:\WINDOWS\system32\ieapfltr.dat,
C:\Documents and Settings\Administrator\Application
Data\Microsoft\IdentityCRL\production\ppcrlconfig.dll,
C:\Documents and Settings\All Users\Application
Data\Microsoft\IdentityCRL\production\ppcrlconfig.dll,
C:\Documents and Settings\Administrator\Application
Data\Microsoft\CryptnetUrlCache\Content\7B2238AA
CCEDC3F1FFE8E7EB5F575EC9,
C:\Documents and Settings\Administrator\Application
Data\Microsoft\CryptnetUrlCache\MetaData\7B2238A
ACCEDC3F1FFE8E7EB5F575EC9,
C:\WINDOWS\system32\xmllite.dll,
C:\Documents and Settings\Administrator\Local
Settings\Application Data\Microsoft\Internet
Explorer\frameiconcache.dat,
C:\Documents and
Settings\Administrator\Favorites\Links\desktop.ini,
C:\Documents and
Settings\Administrator\Favorites\Desktop.ini,
C:\WINDOWS\system32\winhttp.dll,
C:\Program Files\Common Files\Microsoft
Shared\Windows Live\WindowsLiveLogin.dll,
C:\Program Files\Common Files\Microsoft
Shared\Windows Live\msidcrl40.dll
C:\WINDOWS\system32\ieui.dll
C:\WINDOWS\system32\msls31.dll
C:\WINDOWS\system32\ieapfltr.dll
C:\Program Files\Internet Explorer\xpshims.dll
C:\WINDOWS\system32\mshtml.dll
C:\WINDOWS\system32\msfeeds.dll
C:\WINDOWS\system32\activeds.dll
C:\WINDOWS\system32\adsldpc.dll
C:\WINDOWS\system32\credui.dll
C:\WINDOWS\system32\cryptnet.dll
C:\WINDOWS\system32\cscdll.dll
C:\WINDOWS\system32\cscui.dll
C:\WINDOWS\system32\dhcpcsvc.dll
C:\WINDOWS\system32\dot3api.dll
C:\WINDOWS\system32\dot3dlg.dll
C:\WINDOWS\system32\eapolqec.dll
C:\WINDOWS\system32\eappcfg.dll
C:\WINDOWS\system32\eappprxy.dll
C:\WINDOWS\system32\esent.dll
C:\WINDOWS\system32\mprapi.dll
C:\WINDOWS\system32\msxml3r.dll
C:\WINDOWS\system32\netman.dll
C:\WINDOWS\system32\netshell.dll
C:\WINDOWS\system32\onex.dll
C:\WINDOWS\system32\psapi.dll
C:\WINDOWS\system32\qutil.dll
C:\WINDOWS\system32\rasadhlp.dll
C:\WINDOWS\system32\rsaenh.dll
C:\WINDOWS\system32\winlogon.exe

C:\WINDOWS\system32\winrnr.dll
C:\WINDOWS\system32\wintrust.dll
C:\WINDOWS\system32\wmi.dll
C:\WINDOWS\system32\wtsapi32.dll
C:\WINDOWS\system32\wzcsapi.dll
C:\WINDOWS\system32\wzcsvc.dll
C:\Program Files\Messenger\msmsgs.exe
C:\WINDOWS\system32\mswsock.dll
C:\WINDOWS\system32\msxml3.dll
C:\WINDOWS\system32\atl.dll
C:\Program Files\Internet Explorer\sqmapi.dll
C:\WINDOWS\system32\schannel.dll
C:\WINDOWS\AppPatch\aclayers.dll
C:\WINDOWS\system32\urlmon.dll
C:\Program Files\Internet Explorer\ieproxy.dll
C:\WINDOWS\system32\iertutil.dll
C:\WINDOWS\system32\ieframe.dll
C:\WINDOWS\system32\actxprxy.dll
C:\WINDOWS\system32\apphelp.dll
C:\WINDOWS\system32\crypt32.dll
C:\WINDOWS\system32\cryptdll.dll
C:\WINDOWS\system32\digest.dll
C:\WINDOWS\system32\iphlpapi.dll
C:\WINDOWS\system32\ir32_32.dll
C:\WINDOWS\system32\ir41_32.ax
C:\WINDOWS\system32\ir41_qc.dll
C:\WINDOWS\system32\ir41_qcx.dll
C:\WINDOWS\system32\ir50_32.dll
C:\WINDOWS\system32\ir50_qc.dll
C:\WINDOWS\system32\ir50_qcx.dll
C:\WINDOWS\system32\mlang.dll
C:\WINDOWS\system32\msapsspc.dll
C:\WINDOWS\system32\msisip.dll
C:\WINDOWS\system32\msnsspc.dll
C:\WINDOWS\system32\msvcrt40.dll
C:\WINDOWS\system32\rasapi32.dll
C:\WINDOWS\system32\rasman.dll
C:\WINDOWS\system32\rtutils.dll
C:\WINDOWS\system32\sensapi.dll
C:\WINDOWS\system32\setupapi.dll
C:\WINDOWS\system32\sxs.dll
C:\WINDOWS\system32\tapi32.dll
C:\WINDOWS\system32\winspool.drv
C:\WINDOWS\system32\ws2_32.dll
C:\WINDOWS\system32\ws2help.dll
C:\WINDOWS\system32\xpsp2res.dll
C:\WINDOWS\system32\msv1_0.dll
C:\WINDOWS\system32\msasn1.dll
C:\WINDOWS\system32\wshext.dll
C:\WINDOWS\system32\dnsapi.dll
C:\Documents and
Settings\Administrator\Cookies\administrator@live[1].txt
C:\Documents and
Settings\Administrator\Cookies\administrator@msn[1].txt

Protecting Digital Evidence Integrity by Using Smart Cards

Shahzad Saleem and Oliver Popov

Department of Computer and Systems Sciences, DSV Stockholm University
Forum 100, SE-164 40 Kista, Sweden
shahzads@dsv.su.se, popov@dsv.su.se

Abstract. RFC 3227 provides general guidelines for digital evidence collection and archiving, while the International Organization on Computer Evidence offers guidelines for best practice in the digital forensic examination. In the light of these guidelines we will analyze integrity protection mechanism provided by EnCase and FTK which is mainly based on Message Digest Codes (MDCs). MDCs for integrity protection are not tamper proof, hence they can be forged. With the proposed model for protecting digital evidence integrity by using smart cards (PIDESC) that establishes a secure platform for digitally signing the MDC (in general for a whole range of cryptographic services) in combination with Public Key Cryptography (PKC), one can show that this weakness might be overcome.

Keywords: Digital Evidence, Integrity Protection, Smart Card, Message Digest, Digital Signature, Forensics Examination Tools and Procedures.

1 Introduction

RFC 3227 [1] and IOCE's guidelines [2] describe the procedures of forensic examination with an emphasis on gathering and preserving digital evidence. Indeed, RFC 3227 outlines the entire process of collection and archiving digital evidence starting from the principles that should be observed during evidence collection to the tools eventually required. One of the major things stressed in the RFC document is the need for tools that would ensure integrity of the collected and archived digital evidence such as programs to generate checksums and signatures. The implication is obvious, namely even if all the prior steps follow the recommendations; integrity of the evidence is not necessarily protected. This makes protection of the integrity one of the key elements in digital evidence preservation.

Several vulnerabilities and methods to forge integrity have been discussed in [3] [4] [5] [6] [7] [8]. Moreover, message digests alone are not enough to ensure integrity [8], as one can forge them. Considering these factors, one of the solutions to protect integrity of digital evidence is proposed by Seokhee Lee [8] which depends on digital signatures as shown in Figure 1.

I. Baggili (Ed.): ICDF2C 2010, LNICST 53, pp. 110–119, 2011.

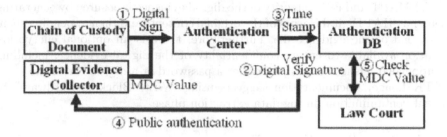

Fig. 1. MAC Authentication Method Scheme [8]

This scheme relies on an assumption that no one can generate a proper and verifiable digital signature without knowing the private key of a relevant entity. When an insecure environment such as a PC is used for safekeeping and/or using private key for cryptography services then there is a possibility that an adversary can steal it. Hence, the core assumption of the scheme is undermined and so is the trust in digital signatures, which points towards the necessity of keeping and using private keys in a secure environment.

It appears that the concept of a Smartcard is an excellent candidate for the aforementioned secure environment. As Smart Card Alliance (SCA) points out that, [9] *"Smart Card is a device with its own embedded integrated circuit chip acting as a secure micro controller with internal memory"*. It connects intelligently and securely to a card reader for storing and or carrying out on-card processing such as encryption, decryption, signing, verification and authentication etc. Smart card technology conforms to international standards ISO/IEC 7816 and 14443.

This paper is organized in seven sections including references. While the current, first, section explains the problem and provides the basic idea behind our approach and solution to the problem of digital evidence integrity protection, second and third sections deal with the current practices and their shortcoming. Then we proceed explaining our model (or solution) PIDESC and how it works. Fifth section analyses the proposed solution and contrasts it with other solutions present in the market against several criteria that range from cost to time complexity. The paper ends with the conclusions and some directions on possibilities for continuing this work in the future.

2   Current Practices for Integrity Protection

A brief discussion of the integrity protection offered by FTK Imager 2.9 [10] and Encase [11] is the subject of this section.

2.1   Integrity Protection by FTK Imager 2.9

FTK Imager 2.9 [10] facilitates forensic extraction of an image of a whole drive or contents of a folder and then exports it into four different formats namely AD1,

RAW, SMART and E01. Integrity of the digital evidence is ensured by generating MD5 and SHA1 Digital Hashes of the original contents and then appending them at the end of the evidence file. Furthermore, there is an optional encryption operation available to ensure confidentiality of the digital evidence; including the appended hashes based upon either a password or a digital certificate.

FTK Imager documentation suggests using "Write Blocking Hardware" to prevent contamination during data extraction phase.

2.2   Integrity Protection by Encase

EnCase [11] provides a tool to forensically extract an image of whole drive and then save it in E01 format. Integrity of the evidence is ensured by CRC and Digital Hashes such as MD5 and SHA1. Optionally, the digital evidence can also be protected by a password providing confidentiality services to the underlying data.

EnCase, like FTK, suggests using "Write Blocking Hardware" to prevent any contamination during data extraction phase.

3   Problems with Current Practices

As underlined in Section 2, current practices employ CRC and digital hashes to ensure integrity and optional password or certificate based encryption and password protection to ensure confidentiality of the digital evidence and its associated MDCs. These practices can be employed in the following scenarios:

1. Only integrity services are turned on by using digital hashes and CRCs. Following instance scenarios can be discussed in this case:
    1.1 Digital Hashes alone are used to ensure Integrity of Digital Evidence as employed by FTK Imager. The intent is to show that it is fairly easy to modify the contents, regenerate the hash value, and replace the original hash with the modified one. The procedure is following:
        i. Digital evidence is extracted from a USB stick which contained a file with information about "heroin" deal.
        ii. The word "heroin" is replaced with "sugar"; then the digital evidence is extracted again and the original values in the appropriate loci of original digital evidence file are replaced with the values from corresponding loci of modified digital evidence file which included data items and digital hashes leaving the original time stamps intact.
        iii. When the modified digital evidence is opened one could notice that the modification went undetected.
    1.2 Digital Hashes and CRC are used together to ensure integrity of digital evidence, where CRC is used to ensure integrity at block level and digital hash is used to ensure integrity for all the digital evidence.
        In this scenario, compromising the integrity of the digital evidence is more difficult than the previous case. However, it is still possible to modify the digital evidence without being detected. Namely, we modified

the contents of digital evidence and then CRC was recomputed for the modified blocks. The same was done with the digital hashes for the modified contents and replaced effected CRCs and Digital Hashes with the modified one.

The experiment was repeated with the addition of CRCs and produced the same results.

2. Digital hashes and CRCs are used to ensure integrity, while symmetric or asymmetric encryption or password protection is used to provide confidentiality services. This scenario can be further divided into two different cases:

2.1 Digital hashes are used for integrity protection and:

2.1.1 Symmetric encryption is used to provide confidentiality to digital evidence including the digital hashes appended with it such as by using a password as a secret key in FTK Imager 2.9. The problem of modification is harder than the previous scenario (both cases), but it is still possible. The underlying security assumption in this case is that an unintended person will not get hold of the secret key. However, a person with sufficient knowledge and tools can steal or guess the secret key. Passwords used as secret keys in FTK Imager 2.9 and possibility of their compromise is further discussed in the section "Attacks on Passwords."

2.1.2 Asymmetric encryption is used to provide confidentiality to digital evidence including the digital hashes appended with it. This case is more difficult for attackers than the previous one i.e. 2.1.1. The assumption is that digital certificates are stored in a computer via appropriate software. A user must enter a password to unlock and open the features of the software that is safe guarding digital certificates. The implication is that if someone knows the password used to start the software and can eventually get an access to the stored certificates then he can use them. So this case is reduced to the one examined above denoted with 2.1.1. The safekeeping and security of the password and their subversion by an un-wanted person is discussed in the section "Attacks on Passwords".

3. Digital signatures are used for integrity protection as suggested by [8].Since we are using software based techniques for safekeeping digital credentials, so the case reduces to 2.1.2 or the possibility to modify digital evidence without being detected.

3.1   Attacks on Passwords

One can find the passwords used in above scenarios by employing different strategies such as social engineering techniques (Shoulder Surfing, Dumpster Diving) and other more sophisticated techniques such as the analysis of RAM and virtual memory.

As an experiment, we attacked the password used by Nexus Personal 4.10.2 [12]. The clients of Handelsbanken [13] use this software to maintain and utilize their private and public key certificates securely. The program works with Internet Browsers such as Internet Explorer, Firefox, Google Chrome, and Flock providing online and internet banking benefits to the Handelsbanken customers.

Encase 6 package was used to capture the contents of the RAM and the contents of Flock Process respectively. Then we analyzed the data to find the password used by Nexus Personal, which was in plain text. In similar manner, pagefile.sys is used as a swap area in Windows operating system. Contents analysis of this file can also reveal the password in plain text.

Hyberfil.sys is used to dump the contents of main memory when system goes on hibernation in Windows. Analyzing the contents of this file can also reveal the password in plain text. There are other artifacts of user activity which can hold clues to the passwords used by such secure stores e.g. Registry Hives, NTUSER.dat etc.

By using the enumerated techniques an illegitimate entity can get hold of a password without being noticed and detected by the legitimate user. This undermines the core security assumption in this paradigm which leaves the Digital Evidence vulnerable to integrity losses.

Nexus Personal is one of the softwares which can be employed to maintain and use digital credentials securely while conducting forensic examination. Our experiments demonstrated that it is not always secure to use software based techniques to store and use digital credentials. This is particularly important when one deals with the probative aspects of digital evidence that can cause significant financial losses and even put human life in peril.

4   The Solution Based on the PIDESC Model

The essence of our proposal, and hence the core of the PIDESC model, is the use of smart cards technology for keeping or maintaining and using digital credentials securely while conducting forensic examination.

The fundamental security assumption in the model is that the loss of smart card will not go undetected. First, it is really hard for an adversary to steal digital credentials from a smart card without stealing the card itself. Stealing a physical entity without being noticed is difficult enough. Moreover, if someone succeeds in stealing a card without being noticed then its absence should be felt by its legitimate user soon enough. The legitimate user can then revoke the keys inside the lost card thus rendering the card useless for any future use.

Following guidelines and standards are considered in solving the problem of integrity protection:

1. Quality Assurance section of IOCE's Guidelines [2] suggests that an organization involved in Forensics Examination should outline and enforce "Competence Requirements" and "Proficiency Testing".
2. Section 5.1.E in IOCE's Guidelines [2] suggests that "An individual is responsible for all the actions taken by him on the digital evidence while it was in his procession."

3. Human intervention should be avoided as much as possible to reduce errors and automated tools should be used as much as possible to produce precise results. It is mandatory that reviewers can assess and evaluate the automated tools being used.
4. Sections 4 and 5 of RFC 3227 [1].

4.1   Pre-conditions

1. PKI is up and running.
2. The organization responsible for the forensic investigation, will issue a smart card to the forensic examiner with his digital credentials embedded in it. Validity of these digital certificates depend on examiner's competence, results of proficiency testing as mandated by "Quality Assurance" section outlined in IOCE's guidelines and other attributes such as time etc.
3. Automated evidence collection tools should be enhanced by adding a service for digital signatures in conjunction with a smart card. This implies that the tool should be able to communicate with a smart card for cryptographic services.
4. Automated evidence collection tool would not operate without initially being able to authenticate its user based on the credentials in the smart card.
5. The tool should be able to communicate with the back end authentication server in the organization and various PKI components.

4.2   Procedure

Following steps are recommended in order to establish strong integrity protection relative to the extracted digital evidence.

1. The forensic examiner should:
   (a) First authenticate himself to the automated forensic tool by using smart card.
   (b) Indicate the tool from where to extract the digital evidence by providing complete description of the corresponding configuration settings.
2. From here automated tool should take control and extract the digital evidence, then
   (a) It should create a digital hash of the contents of digital evidence.
   (b) Tool should communicate with Smart Card to digitally sign the hash obtained from the step above. This Digital Signature Process should also consider information about where, when and by whom the evidence was discovered and extracted thus satisfying a part of requirement outlined in section 4.1 of RFC 3227 (this part requires more research for standardization of format and procedure to incorporate this information into digital signature). Smart card should take this required information from the Digital Credentials saved in it thus reducing examiner's intervention.
   (c) Tool should append this digital signature to the extracted digital evidence.

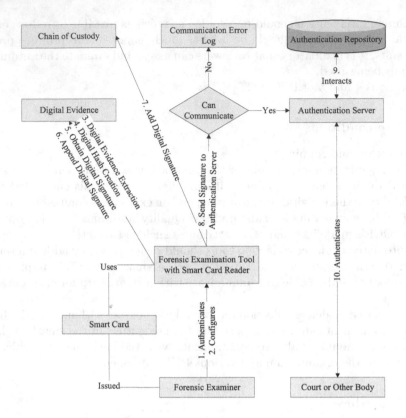

Fig. 2. The PIDESC model and the way it works

(d) Tool should also add this signature to the chain of custody document.
(e) Tool should send the digital signature to organization's authentication server using a secured channel.
(f) If the tool is not able to communicate with the back end server (for instance due to non availability of any communication medium) then it should log the executed processes and list all the reasons for not being able to communicate along with the corresponding time stamps.
3. Authentication server should add a timestamp indicating reception time of digital signature and then store it to the repository of signatures.
4. The organization, institution or any other body which may require verifying integrity of the digital evidence should contact the organization's authentication server of the investigation organization and proceed with the verification.

5   Analysis of Proposed Solution with the PIDESC Model

Results of the analysis of our proposed solution, namely the application of the PIDESC model while considering current practices and other solutions are provided in Table 1. We have used following criteria: upfront cost, operational cost, time, integrity protection, and non-repudiation. The attribution of "+" indicates presence and "-" absence of the criteria under discussion, while the number of "+" indicates the degree of presence. Obviously, a higher the number of "+" signs corresponds to a better performance of the model with respect to the specific criteria.

Table 1. Analysis of current practices and PIDESC model

	Digital Hash Only	Digital Hash with Symmetric Encryption	Digital Hash with Asymmetric Encryption	Digital Signature with Smart Card
Upfront Cost	+	+	+++	+++
Operational Cost	+	+	+++	+++
Time	+	+	++	++
Integrity Protection	+	++	+++	++++
Non-Repudiation	-	-	-	++++

One can clearly notice from the evaluation table that the PIDESC model:

1. Provides better integrity protection as compared with digital hashes or digital signatures (where digital certificates are in the provenance of software based techniques). This is because of the fact that smart cards utilize all across the board secure environment for digital credentials. Hence it is rather difficult for an adversary to manipulate with the integrity of digital evidence.
2. Renowned tools in the industry such as FTK and EnCase use digital hashes alone or encrypted with a secret key to protect integrity of extracted digital evidence. Time required to generate[1] SHA1 Digital Hash on 8 GB USB drive was $1.21 * 10^5$ milliseconds. As depicted in Figure 3, time required to generate[2] a digital signature on SHA1 output is only 0.5 milliseconds which is negligible when compared with the time required to generate a hash. Simply, there is almost no increase in time complexity of the computational requirements compared to current practices.

    Figure 3 represents time in milliseconds required to generate digital signature on 128 bits of SHA1 output, compared with the time required to generate digital hash for 8 and 2 GB USB drives.
3. The model requires PKI. Establishing and operating a PKI is financially demanding. So one could think that PIDESC will require higher upfront costs. But, FTK Imager 2.9 can optionally use digital certificate to provide confidentiality services which mean the prevailing solutions are already moving towards asymmetric cryptography (AC). AC requires PKI at its back end. So, at the present there are situations (and a lot more expected) where people are making serious financial commitments to establish and operate PKI.

---

[1] Using FSUM 2.52, http://www.slavasoft.com/fsum
[2] Using FIPS 201 Standard, Precise Biometric Card Reader with its APIs and Gemalto Smart Card.

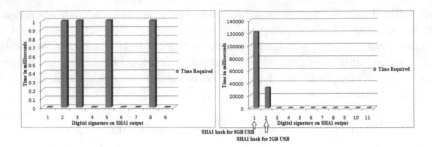

Fig. 3. Time in Milliseconds Required to Generate Signature for 128 bits of SHA1 Output and Time Required to Generate Digital Hash for 8GB and 2 GB USB Drive

4. All the operations such as extraction of digital evidence, generation of digital signature, appending it to the digital evidence, adding it to the chain of custody and communicating it with the backend authentication server, are transparent to the forensic examiner so there is minimal human intervention during most of the phases when the model is running. This indicates that it is:
   (a) Easy for an examiner to operate the tool because of automation.
   (b) Less prone to human errors.
   (c) Provides precise results.
   (d) Fairly open to reviews for consistency, precision and accuracy, which will result in trustworthy digital evidences.
5. There are also additional benefits, or some extra information while generating digital signature such as when, where and who interacted with the digital evidence. This makes repudiation harder and attribution easier.

6   Conclusion

Our work and the paper address and investigate current practices employed to ensure integrity of extracted digital evidence. In order to improve on these practices we have explored and outlined the associated vulnerabilities present in them. Several experiments were conducted to exploit these vulnerabilities which showed that an adversary is able to modify the contents of digital evidence without being detected.

Consequently, we proposed a new model for strong integrity protection of digital evidence using smart cards termed as PIDESC. We proceeded with the critical analysis of the new model in terms of improvements achieved and cost incurred. We found that with a very modest additional cost, the PIDESC model can provide better protection to the integrity of digital evidence along with an additional non-repudiation service, and thus better conformity to the RFC 3227 and IOCE's guidelines.

It is to expect that future work will focus upon the format and data structures needed to communicate information to and from the smart card, such as digital hash, where, when and who interacted with the digital evidence. Indeed, proper and well defined communications and the corresponding environment between the main factors in the secure and with the strong integrity protected digital evidence extraction and collection such as the forensic tool, authentication server, the legal and other bodies that require this evidence is another direction for our research.

References

1. Brezinski, D., Killalea, T.: RFC3227: Guidelines for Evidence Collection and Archiving. RFC Editor United States (2002)
2. International Organization on Computer Evidence (IOCE), Guidelines for best practice in the forensic examination of digital technology, Orlando (2002)
3. Aoki, K., Guo, J., Matusiewicz, K., Sasaki, Y., Wang, L.: Preimages for Step-Reduced SHA-2. In: Matsui, M. (ed.) ASIACRYPT 2009. LNCS, vol. 5912, pp. 578–597. Springer, Heidelberg (2009)
4. Robshaw, M.: On recent results for MD2, MD4 and MD5. RSA Laboratories Bulletin 4 (1996)
5. Stevens, M.: Fast collision attack on MD5. IACR ePrint archive Report 104, 17 (2006)
6. Wang, X., Yin, Y.L., Yu, H.: Finding collisions in the full SHA-1. In: Shoup, V. (ed.) CRYPTO 2005. LNCS, vol. 3621, pp. 17–36. Springer, Heidelberg (2005)
7. Wang, X., Yu, H.: How to break MD5 and other hash functions. In: Cramer, R. (ed.) EUROCRYPT 2005. LNCS, vol. 3494, pp. 19–35. Springer, Heidelberg (2005)
8. Lee, S., Kim, H., Lee, S., Lim, J.: Digital evidence collection process in integrity and memory information gathering. In: First International Workshop on Systematic Approaches to Digital Forensic Engineering, Systematic Approaches to Digital Forensic Engineering, Taipei, Taiwan, pp. 236–247. IEEE, Los Alamitos (2005)
9. Smart card: Introduction: Primer (March 2010),
    http://www.smartcardalliance.org/pages/smart-cards-intro-primer
10. Product downloads (April 2010), http://www.accessdata.com/downloads.html
11. Encase forensic (March 2010), http://www.guidancesoftware.com/default.aspx
12. Nexus personal security client (April 2010),
    http://www.nexussafe.com/en/Products/Nexus-Personal/
13. Handelsbanken (April 2010), http://www.handelsbanken.se

An Architecture for
the Forensic Analysis of Windows System Artifacts

Noor Hashim and Iain Sutherland

Faculty of Advanced Technology, University of Glamorgan, United Kingdom
{nhashim,isutherl}@glam.ac.uk

Abstract. We propose an architecture to enable the forensic investigator to analyze and visualise a range of system generated artifacts with known and unknown data structures. The architecture is intended to facilitate the extraction and analysis of operating system artifacts while being extensible, flexible and reusable. The examples selected for the paper are the Windows Event Logs and Swap Files. Event logs can reveal evidence regarding logons, authentication, accounts and privileged use and can address questions relating to which user accounts were being used and which machines were accessed. The Swap file may contain fragments of data, remnants or entire documents, e-mail messages or the results of internet browsing which may reveal past user activities. Issues relating to understanding and visualising artifacts data structures are discussed and possible solutions are explored. We outline a proposed solution; an extraction component responsible for extracting data and preparing the data for visualisation, a storage subsystem consisting of a database that holds all of the extracted data and the interface, an integrated set of visualization tools.

Keywords: Forensics, Visualisation, Open platform.

1 Introduction

In searching for evidence as part of the forensic process, considerable effort is focused on exploring the contents of the file system and any deleted material that may reside on the media. This will often involve keywords or pattern matching techniques to examine data based on names, content or metadata possibly relating to temporal information, such as the last accessed or written time to be listed [4]. The results therefore can be file content, data fragments and metadata. The investigator can follow a forensic process model to aid the investigation. A forensic process model can be described as follows: for each file, perform a number of type-specific operations such as indexing, keyword searches and thumbnail generation. Thus, the model applies to evidence such as deleted files, file slack, registries, directories and other operating system structures that includes system artifacts. The challenge in digital forensics is to find and discover forensically interesting, suspicious or useful patterns within often very large data sets [2].

I. Baggili (Ed.): ICDF2C 2010, LNICST 53, pp. 120–128, 2011.
© Institute for Computer Sciences, Social Informatics and Telecommunications Engineering 2011

2 Forensic Analysis of Windows System Artifacts

A digital forensic investigation of a hard drive can involve analyzing a large volume of evidence derived from numerous files, directories, unallocated space and file systems [13]. Therefore the forensic analysis of Windows system generated artifacts can be one of many different activities undertaken during a digital forensic investigation. Previous authors [2] have commented on digital forensics' unique requirements and these have to be considered when analyzing Windows system artifacts. These include; the relationship between instances of data, data sources and the issue of false negatives when executing a search over a large volume of data.

3 Windows System Artifacts

There are a number of system generated files of potential evidential value; hidden files, web artifacts, temporary and system files. System files are created as a routine function of the operating system and often without reference to the user. These artifacts are therefore important for digital investigators as they capture a user's activities, but are often overlooked by users if they attempt to conceal or remove evidence of their activities. System files are normally obscured from the average user and require specific knowledge to find and in some cases are only visible or accessible if specialized tools are used. Therefore there should be an element of the forensic process that is focused on capturing and analyzing the information contained in these files.

Table 1. Windows System Artifacts

Event Logs - Event log files record information about which users have been accessing specific files, successfully logging on to a system, unsuccessfully to log on to a system, track usage of specific applications, track alterations to the audit policy, and track changes to user permissions [10].
Swap File - A swap file is a disk-based file under the exclusive control of the Memory Manager [16].
Registry - A central hierarchal database that maintains configuration settings for applications, hardware devices and users. [5].
Recycle Bin – Part of the file system that contains files no longer required by the user. A user may then retrieve a file that has been deleted by mistake, providing the Recycle Bin has not be emptied (placing the file in unallocated space) [6].
Web Cache - Web browsers e.g: Internet Explorer cache the content of visited web pages and cookies within system files. In the case of IE named index.dat [8].
Prefetch - Prefetch caches take information from the boot process and from Scheduled Tasks to speed up boot and application launch time [7].

Based on existing studies [1], [5], [6], [8], [10], [12], analysis of system artifacts play significant role in informing a digital investigation [1], [5]. The ease with which these systems artifacts can be accessed and interpreted depends upon the degree of structure and the form of encoding used in that particular artifact. In some cases the information is stored in plain text, in a highly structured human readable fashion. In other cases, as these files are not intended to be access by the user the system files, they may be encoded and the structure may be unclear without a degree of processing and interpretation. Table 1 includes a brief description of six artifacts represent example of Windows system artifacts.

3.1 Event Logs Evidentiary Values, Features, Tools and Related Issues

Event logs records contain a significant degree of information concerning the activities that occur on a system. They are used to diagnose and troubleshoot issues on a system as they record information about hardware and software problems. According to [10], by reviewing Event logs, a variety of information of evidentiary value can be obtained: they may record successful and unsuccessful logon attempts, user access to specific files, track usage of specific applications, track alterations to the audit policy and track changes to user permissions.

In one example relating to access across a network, Date, Time, IP addresses and Computer Names can be used to determine which computer was used to perform a specific action [6]. Therefore event logs can play an important role in addressing intrusion cases relating for example to the misuse of remote desktop connections. The Event ID column contains a number that indicates the type of event that has occurred. The Event ID is most commonly associated with logon and authentication activity. The Event ID can also be useful in identifying the name and IP address of the computer where the connection originated.

Windows systems record the event that occur on a system into one of three log files: AppEvent.Evt, SecEvent.Evt and SysEvent.Evt. These three files record within many facets of a systems behavior.

Table 2. Event Logs Organisation

File Name	File Location For Windows NT/XP, 2000, Vista
Application Event Log AppEvent.Evt	Contains a log of application usage and logged messages from the operating system and programs. %SYSTEMROOT%\system32\config\
Security Event Log SecEvent.Evt	Records activities that have security implications such as logins. %SYSTEMROOT%\WINNT\config\
System Event Log SysEvent.Evt	Notes system events such as shutdowns. %SystemRoot%\system32\winevt\Logs

Table 2 illustrates the different locations that the various versions of Windows store the .Evt file. According to [1], in order to facilitate the examination of the contents of an event log, the event log header and event records have some structure, values and information that can assist an investigator in recognizing and interpreting the files. These values include date, time, user, computer, event ID, source, type and category [11]. It is maintained as a circular buffer where older event records are overwritten once the file reaches a specified size and when a new event record is added to the file. At the same time, there is correlation between the event logs, registry and many of message files (DLL) on a system [5].

Information, warning and error entries are stored in the Application and System logs, while success and failure are recorded in the Security log. This type of event is frequently used in attempts to troubleshoot system anomalies and used with other column fields to determine evidence of a breach, or attempted breach of the computer system. In Windows, each of the different versions of the operating systems used logon type to indicate different kind of logon event and these nine logon types are values to indicate the way in which the account logged on to the system.

Since these logs are stored in a proprietary binary format and not in a Human readable format, appropriate tools are required to access and interpret the data. Event Viewer by Microsoft is one example. This depicts the event logs in two different panes. One pane shows the list of the available log files and the other provides a list of each different event entry. Other tools that rely on the Windows API is 'Log Parser'. For Log Parser the processing of event logs is done by three engines: its input engine, its SQL engine (which uses SQL queries to parse, filter and analyze logs) and its output engine. LANguard Security Event Log Monitor (LANSELM, from GFI) is a network-wide tool that retrieves events from NT/2000 servers and workstations and alert the administrator of possible intrusions.

One important element of forensic value is the timestamp. Event logs record the date the entry was made and the time entry was written in the log. Windows stores timestamps in FILETIME format and in GMT but does not contain any information concerning the time zone. Therefore, when comparing a timestamp with another system, in addition to compensating for any clock variation, differences in time zones may have to be considered.

Another issue is the data loss that occurs when an event ID has been updated on a newer version of the operating system, and an older version of the operating system is used to interpret the event log files. This problem also arises in relation to SIDs when a log from a different computer is analyzed instead of local machine. The evolution of Windows operating system also creates problems as it has resulted in changes to the way that logs are generated, the evidence found would therefore be a consequence of the version of the operating system that a victim is using.

3.2 Swap File Evidentiary Values, Features, Tools and Related Issues

The swap file is a portion of disk storage used for memory pages belonging to various processes [9] and threads [15] and also stores CrashDump data when a "blue screen of death" occurs [14]. This swap file can provide a great deal of information, specifically passwords [6], [9], user IDs and information that the user did not intend to save to the disk. The later could include chat information, credit card numbers, URLs, print spooling and numerous other user activities [13].

When a computer's RAM is full, the operating system allocates memory for an application, Windows creates swap files on the root folder of the system drive to make more RAM available. The default swap file location is as shown in Table 3. The Swap file is generated at each boot session and is closed on system shutdown. However, the shutdown period increases when the swap file is configured to clear out by setting the registry value to 1 for: HKEY_LOCAL_MACHINE\SYSTEM\Current Control-Set\Control\SessionManager\MemoryManagement\ClearPageFileAtShutdown.

The swap file is locked by the kernel when Windows is running. However, it is possible to access the swap file either by using a specially written driver or by accessing the swap file by removing the files from a 'cold' system, by forensically imaging the hard drive. The swap file size depends on the volume of RAM present on the system and how much virtual memory space is required by a particular workload. If the minimum and maximum swap file size is not the same, fragmentation happens and this can lead to performance degradation.

In this project various computer forensic filters were designed to automatically identify string based information present in a Windows swap files.

Table 3. Swap File Default Name and Location

File Name	Windows Version	Location
Win386.swp	Windows 95/98/ME	%SystemRoot%\
pagefile.sys	Windows NT/2000/XP/Vista	

4   Architecture and System Requirements

The aim of the project is to develop an extensible open source architecture for system generated artifacts. The previous sections highlight the evidential value of these files. The current state of the art forensic tools (EnCase and FTK) are capable of capturing the system-generated files present on a drive. These commercial tools also provide standard features to search and pattern match the contents of these files. However the coverage of system generated artifacts varies; facilities to process and explore the registry tend to be feature rich, whereas those for analyzing swap files and event logs are less well developed. The information on the artifacts above and the functionality provided by the commercial tools provides a baseline for the development of a series of minimum requirements for the proposed architecture.

4.1   Functional Requirements

The following functional requirements have been indentified: The need to automate the analysis of system artifacts (extraction, processing and presentation) to help the investigator to explore and understand the content of the files. There is also a requirement to facilitate the analysis and visualization of forensic data from various types of file format and data with different degrees of complexity. The system will need to be able to understand the variation between different versions of the operating system, to analyze evidence items collected from different platforms. The system will also need to present and summaries the information of interest for reporting purposes.

4.2   Security, Software Quality and Other Requirements

In terms of security and other requirements the following have been identified. As a forensics tool, data integrity is essential and the original copies of the data / media must remain unchanged and this should be verifiable. Some form of hashing function (MD5, SHA-1 or similar) is required to prove that the evidence has not been modifed.

A further particularly essential requirement for a forensics tool is accuracy. The accuracy of the generated information output from the analyzed files and shown using textual visualization technique is of paramount importance.

The system should be both reliable with stable, repeatable performance and scalable to add visualization techniques capability to additional evidence items as the need arises. In term of extensibility the following two requirements were identified:

- Extensibility-1: It is easy to add support for new types of data sources regarding analysis.
- Extensibility-2: Additional functionality can be added through plugins or modules, as well as scripting capability via an extensive and usable API.

The extensibility should also support dynamic reconfiguration, modifications and enhancements must be possible without taking the whole system down and implementation should be independent of underlying software.

Confidentiality is important and methods shall be considered to protect data within the evidence item from being disclosed to unintended parties. Finally there should be some form of integrity assurance. To provide audit record about timestamp or actions taken, or results returned from running utilities.

5   System Architecture

This research concentrates on the examination of the system artifacts' data structures and transforming the data into structured form, thereby helping the investigator by automating the time consuming aspect of low-level analysis of the system file format and related data complexity. The basic approach consists of these four steps:

The first step is to prepare the artifacts to be processed. The artifact to be processed comes in one of these formats: exported from imaged hard drive using tools such as Mount Image Pro or FTK, acquired from Digital Evidence Bag container of digital evidence obtained from disparate sources, stored using the Advanced Forensics Format (AFF) to indicate imaged disk storage and compressed data used to store digital evidence.

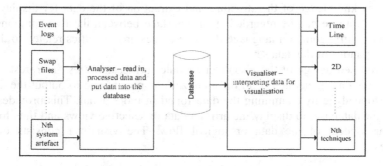

Fig. 1. High Level Description of Overall Architecture

The second step will be to invoke analyzer to identify and extract data in each of the artifacts being processed. The analyzer will need to be easily reconfigurable to interpret the variety of artifacts.

The third step is to invoke the database as a data store that enables data to be queried and retrieved.

The fourth step in the process is to transform the data into an easily readable format. It is a mechanism where data is queried from the database, data representation and further analysis. This is used to structure the data into a narrative construct.

The top-level design of the Windows System Artifacts Analysis system is shown in Fig. 1.

5.1 Analyzer, Database and Visualizer

The key features of the proposed system are therefore the analyzer, the database and the visualization system. The analyzer component firstly reads in the evidence item and translates it into usable structure. This performs the automated analysis. Once processed, the data is sent to the database to allow for further future analysis by the operator. The main process of the analyzer consists of five processes:

1. Locate: Locate the fields of the data structure (the units of information that comprise the data structure).
2. Extract: Extract the fields of the data structure from the raw stream of bytes.
3. Decode: Further extraction is necessary, specifically the bit fields. Examples of bit fields are: flags, attributes, date field, time field, etc.
4. Interpretation: Takes the output of the decoding phase or the extraction step and performs various computations using the information. Examples: the value for the years of date field and second of time field need to be interpreted.
5. Reconstruction: Information from the previous step is used to reconstruct a usable representation of the data structure or at least the relevant fields.

Part of the initial system configuration for processing a particular artifact, in addition to providing the analyzer with information on the structure of the artifact, will be configuring the database. The database must be available to store data and this data can be rapidly retrieved and queried. It must be extensible in term of accepting data without any knowledge of the structure and extraction of the data for display or report. This database can be regarded as an interface between the two components to communicate in a common language that overcomes any specifics related to the syntax and semantics of the data set.

The proposed design of the visualizer module further analyzes, interprest and understands the data generated from the analyzer component and to output the data for the user to analyze by examining the data found in more detail. This provides interfaces to the database, to display the artifact data in selective views and thus focus on particular aspects of the data or logical flow. The visualizer consists of eight processes:

1. Acquire: Obtain the data, whether from a file on a disk, or a source over a network.
2. Parse: Provide some structure for the data's meaning.

3. Filter: Remove any irrelevant data.
4. Mine: Apply methods from statistics or data mining as a way to discern patterns or place the data in mathematical context.
5. Represent: Determines the basic form that a set of data will take, such as a graph.
6. Refine: Design methods are used to improve the basic representation to make it clearer and more visually engaging.
7. Interact: Add methods for manipulating the data or controlling what features are visible.
8. Output: The information file is translated into required output format and output to the screen.

6 Conclusion and Future Work

This is a research-in-progress. The contribution lies not on the ability to manipulate and visualize the event logs and swap files, but rather the development of a flexible and extensible architecture to process various artifacts based on a clear understanding of the priority of the requirements.

Forensic analysis has a number of unique requirements that directly impact the design of the architecture. For example, the need to interact with multiple disparate data types suggests the development of plugins and flexibility. The architecture should be able to process other system artifacts (e.g. Registry, Internet Explorer Activity Files, Prefetch file) besides event logs and swap files. Our ongoing work includes the implementation of the architecture to enable it to visualize known and unknown data structure of files. This will enable the investigator to easily determine what data of interest is available within these system areas of Windows.

References

1. Anson, S., Bunting, S.: Mastering Windows Network Forensics and Investigation, Indiana (2007)
2. Brown, R., Palm, B., de Vel, O.: Design of a Digital Forensics Image Mining System (2005), http://www.springerlink.com/content/3a7t7cxk3mdrajb0/
3. Caloyannides, M.A.: Computer Forensics and Privacy, Boston (2001)
4. Carrier, B.: File System Forensic Analysis, Indiana (2005)
5. Carvey, H.: Windows Forensic Analysis DVD Toolkit, Burlington (2007)
6. Casey, E.: Digital Evidence and Computer Crime: Forensic Science, Computers and the Internet, Boston (2004)
7. Hay, S.A.: Windows File Analyzer Guidance (2005), http://www.mitec.cz/Downloads/WFA%20Guidance.pdf
8. Jones, K.J.: Forensic Analysis of Internet Explorer Activity Files, Forensic Analysis of Microsoft Windows Recycle Bin Records (2003)
9. Lee, S., Savoldi, A., Lee, S., Lim, J.: Windows Pagefile Collection and Analysis for a Live Forensics Context. J. Future Gen. Comm. and Net. 2, December 6-8 (2007)
10. Mandia, K., Prosise, C., Pepe, M.: Incident Response & Computer Forensics, New York (2003)

11. Microsoft TechNet: Fundamental Computer Investigation Guide For Windows: Overview (2007)
12. Murphey, R.: Automated Windows event log forensics. J. Digital Investigation 4S, S92–S100 (2007)
13. Nelson, B., Phillips, A., Enfinger, F., Steuart, C.: Guide to Computer Forensics and Investigations (2008)
14. Ruff, N.: Windows Memory Forensics. J. Computer Virology 4S, S92-S100. The British Library (2007)
15. Schuster, A.: Searching For Processes And Threats In Microsoft Windows Memory Dump. J. Digital Investigation 3S, S10–S16 (2006)
16. The NT Insider: Windows NT Virtual Memory. Open System Resources. V. 5, I. 2 (1998), http://www.osronline.com/custom.cfm?name=articlePrint.cfm&id=60

An IP Traceback Model for Network Forensics

Emmanuel S. Pilli, R.C. Joshi, and Rajdeep Niyogi

Department of Electronics and Computer Engineering,
Indian Institute of Techology Roorkee, Roorkee, India
{emshudec,rcjosfec,rajdpfec}@iitr.ernet.in, emmshub@gmail.com

Abstract. Network forensics deals with capture, recording, analysis and investigation of network traffic to traceback the attackers. Its ultimate goal is to provide sufficient evidence to allow the perpetrator to be prosecuted. IP traceback is an important aspect in the investigation process where the real attacker is identified by tracking source address of the attack packets. In this paper we classify the various approaches to network forensics to list the requirements of the traceback. We propose a novel model for traceback based on autonomous systems (AS) and deterministic packet marking (DPM) to enable traceback even with a single packet. The model is analyzed against various evaluation metrics. The traceback solution will be a major step in the direction of attack attribution and investigation.

Keywords: network forensics, traceback, DPM, AS, attack attribution.

1 Introduction

IP traceback problem involves identifying the actual source of a packet across the Internet. Many techniques for traceback have been proposed, but all of them are focused on distributed denial of service (DDoS) attacks [1]. Many of the techniques can be slightly modified or extended for handling other attacks as well.

The weaknesses in TCP/IP facilitate *IP spoofing* where source address in the IP header can be manipulated and an address other than the actual can be placed. The routing infrastructure of the Internet is stateless and hence the reconstruction of the path back to the attacker is a non-trivial task. Network address translation (NAT) and stepping-stone attack also complicate the process. IP traceback mechanisms aim at tracking back the source of attacks. If this is realized, IP traceback will be the major part of investigation phase in network forensics.

We propose to use a two level traceback mechanism based on deterministic packet marking (DPM) using an Autonomous Systems (AS). The first level involves marking of each outgoing packet by the first ingress edge router and the second level involves marking each outgoing packet by the AS edge router (ASER). Packet is marked only once at each level. A single packet is sufficient to detect the source and the model is the first of its kind where DPM and AS marking is taken as a combination.

The paper is organized as follows: Section 2 provides a basis for network forensic approach to traceback. Section 3 makes a survey of existing traceback techniques and identifies a model for network forensics. We propose a model for traceback in Section 4. Conclusion and future work are given in section 5.

I. Baggili (Ed.): ICDF2C 2010, LNICST 53, pp. 129–136, 2011.

2   Assumptions and Requirements for Forensic Traceback

Network forensics is the science that deals with capture, recording, and analysis of network traffic [2]. Network forensic systems are classified [3] into different types, based on various characteristics. We extend two more classes:

- Time of Analysis: *Real time* forensics involves live network security surveillance and monitoring. *Post mortem* investigation of packet captures is done offline.
- Data Source: *Flow based* systems collect statistical information as network traffic flows. *Packet based* systems involve deep packet inspection.

We identify a set of requirements and make necessary assumptions for traceback in the context of network forensics. We limit our work to the post mortem, packet based network forensics.

Assumptions: The number of packets generated for DDoS attacks are huge and many techniques have been designed to exploit this situation. Network forensics may handle attacks which may involve very few packets. The assumptions made for designing traceback mechanisms for DDoS are modified to suit the investigation of cyber crimes. They are given below:

- attackers are able to generate and send any packet
- multiple attackers may act in a coordinated fashion
- attackers are aware of the traceback ability
- routers possess limited processing and storage capabilities
- routers are rarely compromised and all routers may not participate in traceback
- suspicious packet stream may consist of just a few packets

Requirements: Goals for effective and efficient traceback can be designed for evaluating existing traceback solutions and build new mechanisms in the future. Some of the key requirements, specifically to suit network forensics traceback, include the following:

- compatibility with existing network protocols, routers and infrastructure
- simple and minimal number of functions to be implemented on transit routers
- support for incremental implementation, partial deployment and scalability
- minimal overhead of time and resources (processing, bandwidth, memory)
- fast convergence of the traceback process involving a few packets
- minimal involvement of the internet service provider (ISP) in the process

3   IP Traceback

IP Traceback [4, 5] problem is defined as "identifying the actual source of any packet sent across the Internet". The traceback mechanism is shown in Fig. 1. We consider proactive measures applicable only for network forensics like logging, packet marking, hybrid approaches and AS-level traceback techniques.

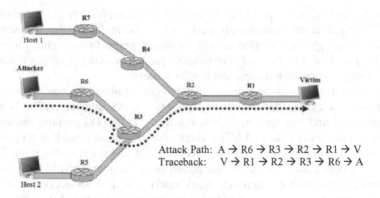

Attack Path: A → R6 → R3 → R2 → R1 → V
Traceback: V → R1 → R2 → R3 → R6 → A

Fig. 1. IP Traceback

3.1 Background

The true origin of an attacker can be identified by *logging* packets at key routers and later mining them for attack path reconstruction. Snoeren et al. [6] proposed *source path isolation engine* (SPIE) capable of tracing a single IP packet. A hash of multiple fields in the IP packet header is computed and logged in the digest tables. Baba and Matsuda [7] propose an *autonomous management network* (AMN), where monitoring manager receives requests from sensors which detect attacks. It queries the tracers maintaining log information about incoming packets to traceback.

Packet-marking involves placing the routers' part or complete address into the IP packet randomly with a fixed probability or only once deterministically. Savage et al. [8] proposed *probabilistic packet marking* (PPM) where each router probabilistically marks the Identification field in the IP packets (one in 25) with partial address information. Song and Perrig [9] proposed *advanced and authenticated packet marking* (AAPM) to reduce the storage space requirements by encoding the IP address into an 8 bit hash value used message authentication codes (MAC) to prevent packet content tampering. Dean et al. [10] proposed *algebraic packet marking* (APM) that employs algebraic techniques from the field of coding theory to calculate the values of 15-bit marks as points on polynomials. Yaar et al. [11] proposed *fast internet traceback* (FIT) that has three elements, a fragment of the hash of the marking router's IP address, the number of the hash fragment marked in the packet, and a distance field. Belenky and Ansari [12] proposed *deterministic packet marking* (DPM) where only the ingress edge routers mark the packets and all other routers are exempt from marking. Rayanchu and Barua [13] propose a *deterministic edge router marking* (DERM) where the 16-bit hash of the IP address is used to mark each packet.

Hybrid traceback approaches integrate packet marking and packet logging in a novel fashion to achieve the advantages of both the techniques. Duwairi and Govindarasu [14] propose *distributed link list traceback* (DLLT) where a router decides to mark the packet, stores the current IP address along with the packet ID in the marking table maintained at the router, and then marks the packet by its own IP address, and forwards the packet. Jing et al. [15] propose *hierarchical IP traceback system* (HITS) with three components for marking, evidence collection and traceback processing.

Gong and Sarac [16] develop *hybrid single packet IP traceback* (HIT) based on marking and logging. Traceback enabled routers audit traffic and a traceback server having the network topology information constructs attack graph by querying routers. Jing and Lin [17] propose *logging and deterministic packet marking* (LDPM) which traces the special edge connecting ingress and border routers.

Autonomous System can be a group of networks regulated by one or more entity, which enforces a clearly defined routing policy. An AS number (ASN) is a 16-bit integer, assigned and managed by IANA. Paruchuri et al. [18] propose *authenticated autonomous system traceback* (AAST) which probabilistically mark packets with AS number at AS Border Routers using 19 bits for ASN and the distance field. Gao and Ansari [19] propose *autonomous system based edge marking* (ASEM) in which only the ingress edge routers of each AS, mark packets with ASN according to certain probability. Packets are not remarked by all other routers. Korkmaz et al. [20] propose *AS-level single packet traceback* (AS-SPT) which logs packet digests at the border routers of participating ASes and traces toward packet origin at the AS-level. Castelucio et al. [21] propose an AS-level overlay network that operates on the border routers of an AS and builds an overlay network after exchanging BGP information.

3.2 Related Work

Focus of the IP Traceback approaches were in mitigating DDoS attacks by identifying the attack traffic and restrict it from reaching the victim. Relation between the major traceback mechanisms is shown in Fig. 2 to identify the suitable model for forensics.

Few researchers have identified the need to perform network traceback for other attacks. Carrier and Shields [22] propose the Session TOken Protocol (STOP) based on the Identification protocol (IDENT) and is aimed to automatically trace attackers logging through a series of stepping stones. Demir et al. [23] propose two approaches, session based packet logging (SBL) and SYN based packet marking (SYNPM), for traceback by providing simple and effective logging. Cohen [24] explores the problem of determining the real source behind the NAT gateway.

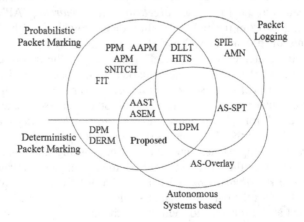

Fig. 2. Relation between various traceback techniques

4 Proposed Model

We propose an IP traceback model for network forensics based on the assumptions and requirements as listed earlier. The architecture is shown in Fig. 3. Our technique is based on deterministic packet marking (DPM) using an Autonomous System (AS) approach. We use a two level traceback mechanism, where the first level involves deterministic marking of each packet by the first ingress edge router within the AS and the second level involves marking each packet by the AS edge router (ASER). In both the levels, once the packet is marked, it cannot be marked by any other router. Every outbound packet is marked and inbound packets are not marked. A single packet is sufficient to detect the source as each contains the information about the AS and the edge router which first marked the packet.

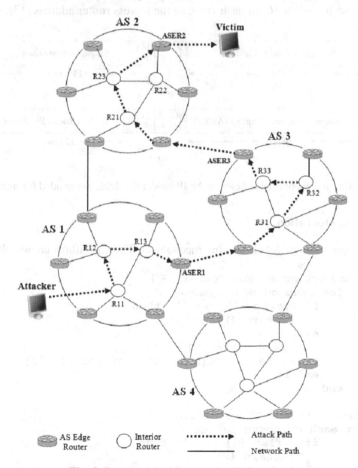

Fig. 3. Proposed Architecture for IP Traceback

4.1 Mark Information Encoding

We propose to use the 16-bit ID field, 3-bit fragment flag field and 13-bit fragment offset field in the IP header to store the marking information. These 32 bits were designed to hold information about fragmentation. The fragmentation traffic is very rare in Internet these days (about 0.25% of all traffic) [16]. The mapping between fields in the IP header and the marking fields is shown in Figure 4.

16 bits of ID field are used to hold the AS number (ASN), a globally unique number used to identify an AS. We use the ASN for marking rather than IP addresses as it is easy to mark it in the available 16 bits and will result in less number of false positives. This type of encoding was also done in [27]. After the marking is done, the reserved flag bit (first bit of the flag field immediately after the ID field) is set to 1.

The next 16 bits following the ID field are made up of 3-bit flag and 13-bit offset field. 12 most significant bits of the 13-bit offset is used to store the hashed IP address of the first ingress router traversed by the packet [18]. The remaining least significant bit is used as a flag to indicate that the marking has taken place. We may also use all the 16 bits also to store a 16-bit hash value of the ingress router address [13].

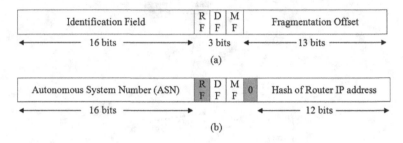

Fig. 4. Marking encoding (a) fields in the IP header (b) fields overloaded for marking

4.2 Marking Operation

We have proposed a two-level marking mechanism. The algorithms are as follows:

```
program MarkIngressEdgeRouter (R_i)
      for each outbound packet P
          if P.offset[0] == '1' then
              forward (P)
          else
              set P.offset[0] == '1'
              write HashIP(R_i) into P.offset [1..12]
          end if
      end for

program MarkASEdgeRouter (ASER_i)
      for each outbound packet P
          if P.flag [0] == '1' then
              forward (P)
          else
              set P.flag [0] == '1'
              write ASN (ASER_i) into P.Identification
              only if P is forwarded to another ASER
          end if
      end for
```

4.3 Traceback Operation

Traceback operation is simple as each packet holds the information required to identify the AS and the first ingress router. The 16-bit identification field in the IP header gives the ASN, identifying the source AS of the packet. The 12-bit hash value in the offset field is used to extract the ingress router IP address using the hash function. This information can be extracted even from a single attack packet.

4.4 Analysis

A *single packet* can give the information till the ingress router to which the attacker was connected. There is *no additional storage* required, neither at the router nor at the victim. None of the packets are logged and nor information about the packets is stored. The *processing overhead is nominal* as the marking operations are simple functions, which can be easily performed. The hashing of router IP addresses can be calculated in advance, stored and be made available when required. The processing overhead may increase when full bandwidth traffic has to be marked. There is very *less infrastructure change* which needs to be made, as marking is done only twice. The technique is *scalable* and can handle many attackers as each attackers information can be given by a single packet. Number of *false positives is less* as the entire information is coded into a single packet. The hashing functions may have collisions yielding a few false positives. There is a *considerable amount of ISP involvement* needed as an AS can be thought of as an ISP. It must make the ASN available for routers to be enabled for traceback. *Incremental deployment is limited* as the marking is done only twice and if some of the routers are not enabled, the technique may yield more false positives.

5 Conclusion

The most challenging problem for network forensics, IP traceback, was examined in this paper. A traceback model based on Autonomous System and Deterministic Packet Marking was proposed. The proposed technique can trace the attacker till the ingress edge router even with a single packet which meets the basic requirement of network forensics. It requires nominal processing and there is no storage overhead. The only drawback is the higher involvement of ISP operating the AS. Future work involves performance analysis using simulations to validate our technique in comparison with the existing traceback techniques. Accommodating fragmentation of packets, while using the 32 bits used for fragmentation to mark packets, is also a challenge.

References

[1] Lee, S.C., Shields, C.: Tracing the Source of Network Attack: A Technical, Legal and Societal Problem. In: IEEE Workshop IAS, New York, pp. 239–246 (2001)
[2] Palmer, G.: A Road Map for Digital Forensic Research. In: Proc. 1st Digital Forensic Research Workshop (DFRWS), pp. 27–30 (2001)
[3] Pilli, E.S., Joshi, R.C., Niyogi, R.: Network forensic frameworks: Survey and research challenges. Digit. Investig, available online March (2010) (in press)

[4] Gao, Z., Ansari, N.: Tracing Cyber Attacks from the Practical Perspective. IEEE Communications Magazine 43(5), 123–131 (2005)

[5] Santhanam, L., Kumar, A., Agrawal, D.P.: Taxonomy of IP Traceback. J. Info. Assurance and Security 1, 79–94 (2006)

[6] Snoeren, A.C., Partridge, C., Sanchez, L.A., Jones, C.E., Tchakoutio, F., Kent, S.T., Strayer, S.T.: Hash-Based IP Traceback. In: Proceedings of ACM SIGCOMM (2001)

[7] Baba, T., Matsuda, S.: Tracing Network Attacks to Their Sources. IEEE Internet Computing, 20–26 (March/April 2002)

[8] Savage, S., Wetherall, D., Karlin, A., Anderson, T.: Network Support for IP Traceback. IEEE/ACM Transactions on Networking 9(3), 226–237 (2001)

[9] Song, D., Perrig, A.: Advanced and Authenticated Marking Schemes for IP Traceback. In: Proceedings of the IEEE INFOCOM 2001, Arkansas, USA (2001)

[10] Dean, D., Franklin, M., Stubblefield, A.: An Algebraic Approach to IP Traceback. ACM Transactions on Information and System Security 5, 119–137 (2002)

[11] Yaar, A., Perrig, A., Song, D.: FIT: Fast Internet Traceback. In: Proc. IEEE 24th Ann. Joint Conf. Computer and Comm. Societies (INFOCOMM 2005), pp. 1395–1407 (2005)

[12] Belenky, A., Ansari, N.: On Deterministic Packet Marking. Computer Networks 51, 732–750 (2006)

[13] Rayanchu, S.K., Barua, G.: Tracing Attackers with Deterministic Edge Router Marking (DERM). In: Ghosh, R.K., Mohanty, H. (eds.) ICDCIT 2004. LNCS, vol. 3347, pp. 400–409. Springer, Heidelberg (2004)

[14] Duwairi, A., Manimaran, G.: Novel Hybrid Schemes Employing Packet Marking and Logging for IP Traceback. IEEE Trans. Parallel and Dist. Sys. 17(5), 403–418 (2006)

[15] Jing, Y.N., Tu, P., Wang, X.P., Zhang, G.D.: Distributed log based scheme. In: Proc of 5th Int'l. Conf. on Computer and Information Technology (2005)

[16] Gong, C., Sarac, K.: A More Practical Approach for Single-Packet IP Traceback using Packet Marking and Logging. IEEE Trans. Parallel and Dist. Sys. 19(10), 1310–1324 (2008)

[17] Jing, W.X., Lin, X.Y.: IP Traceback based on Deterministic Packet Marking and Logging. In: Proc. IEEE Int'l. Conf. on Scalable Computing and Comm., pp. 178–182 (2009)

[18] Paruchuri, V., Durresi, A., Kannan, R., Iyengar, S.S.: Authentic Autonomous Traceback. In: Proc. 18th Int'l Conf. Adv. Info. Networking and Appln., pp. 406–413 (2004)

[19] Gao, Z., Ansari, N.: A practical and robust inter-domain marking scheme for IP traceback. Computer Networks 51(3), 732–750 (2007)

[20] Korkmaz, T., et al.: Single packet IP traceback in AS-level partial deployment scenario. Int. J. Security and Networks 2(1/2), 95–108 (2007)

[21] Castelucio, A., Ziviani, A., Salles, R.M.: An AS-level Overlay Network for IP Traceback. IEEE Network, 36–41 (2009)

[22] Carrier, B., Shields, C.: The Session Token Protocol for Forensics and Traceback. ACM Trans. on Info. System Security 7(3), 333–362 (2004)

[23] Demir, O., Ping, J., Kim, J.: Session Based Packet Marking and Auditing for Network Forensics. Int'l. Journal of Digital Evidence 6(1), 1–15 (2007)

[24] Cohen, M.I.: Source attribution for network address translated forensic captures. Digit. Investig. 5(3-4), 138–145 (2009)

Forensic Data Carving

Digambar Povar and V.K. Bhadran

Center for Development of Advanced Computing, Trivandrum,
Ministry of Communications and Information Technology, Govt. of India
{paward,bhadran}@cdactvm.in

Abstract. File or data carving is a term used in the field of Cyber forensics. Cyber forensics is the process of acquisition, authentication, analysis and documentation of evidence extracted from and/or contained in a computer system, computer network and digital media. Extracting data (file) out of undifferentiated blocks (raw data) is called as carving. Identifying and recovering files based on analysis of file formats is known as file carving. In Cyber Forensics, carving is a helpful technique in finding hidden or deleted files from digital media. A file can be hidden in areas like lost clusters, unallocated clusters and slack space of the disk or digital media. To use this method of extraction, a file should have a standard file signature called a file header (start of the file). A search is performed to locate the file header and continued until the file footer (end of the file) is reached. The data between these two points will be extracted and analyzed to validate the file. The extraction algorithm uses different methods of carving depending on the file formats.

Keywords: Cyber Forensics, Data Carving, Slack Space, Lost and Unallocated Clusters.

1 Introduction

Computer forensics deals with the important problem of recovering files from digital media for which no file system information available [1][2]. The file system information can be unavailable for several reasons. First, digital media can be formatted to destroy the file system. Second, the file of interest may have been deleted such that the file system indexes no longer refer to the file content. Third, digital media may contain an unknown file system. Last, a file can be hidden in areas like lost clusters, unallocated clusters and slack space. In all the above cases, the file content is usually unchanged until the clusters belonging to the file are overwritten with other files. The process of file recovery from digital media by locating file signatures (header, footer) and extracting data between these end points is known as file carving. A file on digital media can start at cluster, sector, or at any byte (only in case of embedded files). To optimize the search process of locating the header signature, it is sufficient to search for the first few bytes of every cluster or sector. In case of embedded files, a search has to be performed byte by byte. The Boyer-Moore string search algorithm is used to perform a byte by byte search. The Boyer-Moore searching algorithm, described in R. S. Boyer and J. S. Moore's 1977 paper *"A Fast String Searching Algorithm"* [3] is among the best ways known for finding a sub string in a search space.

I. Baggili (Ed.): ICDF2C 2010, LNICST 53, pp. 137–148, 2011.
© Institute for Computer Sciences, Social Informatics and Telecommunications Engineering 2011

Using their method it is possible to search a data space for a known pattern without having to examine all the characters in the search space. One or more of the file carving methods proposed by Simson Garfinkel and Joachim Metz [14] are used to carve files depending on the file types. Our Forensic Data Carving method uses the following methods proposed by them.

- ❖ Header/Footer carving
- ❖ Header/Embedded length carving
- ❖ File structure based carving
- ❖ Carving with validation and
- ❖ Header/Maximum file size carving

Each of these methods with suitable example will be described in following sections. Files such as digital images (jpeg, gif, bmp, png), html, zip, compound documents (doc, ppt, excel, thumbs.db), pdf, video (avi, dat, mp4, mov, wmv, 3gp) can be carved using the above mentioned methods. We produced a tool using the methods discussed above. This tool is developed keeping two challenges in mind. First, carving files from hidden areas of the digital media when the file system exists. Second, carving files from any raw image that does or does not have a file system. To carve files from only hidden areas, we implemented a system that is available as a module for Cyber-Check V4.0 (a disk analysis tool). This module provides in-place (or zero storage) carving [14] facility from lost clusters, unallocated clusters and disk slack. It also supports carving files that are embedded into other files such as picture files embedded into documents and thumbs.db which contain picture thumbnails. To carve files from any raw image, we also created a stand-alone tool that can connect to external storage to carve files of interest.

2 An Approach to Minimize Search Time

Traditional forensic data carving tools available today search the header signature of a file in whole forensic image of a given digital media even if the file system exists for the media. To minimize the search space, it is sufficient to search header signatures in lost clusters, unallocated clusters and slack space of the disk that has a file system. Additionally, it is not necessary to search for the header signature of a file that is not embedded into another file in an entire cluster or sector. Any file that is newly created would be allocated a few fresh clusters or sectors and its header signature will be available in the first few bytes of first cluster or sector. Therefore, to minimize the header signature search time we suggest the following search options. Search the header signature in the:

- ❖ Option1: First few bytes of cluster
- ❖ Option2: First few bytes of sector
- ❖ Option3: Throughout the sector

All the above search options can be used for the digital media forensic image with a supported file system. It is important to note that sometimes, using the Option 1 search may lead to missing key evidence. For example, suppose a hard disk is formatted using a FAT32 file system and its cluster size is 2 sectors as shown in following Figure 1.

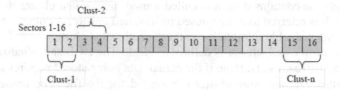

Fig. 1. Media representation with 2 sectors per cluster

If a file is stored in the second cluster, its header signature is stored in first few bytes of the second cluster or third sector. If the same hard disk is formatted and its cluster size is 4 sectors as shown in Figure 2, this search option misses the file starting at sector 3. This problem may be resolved by using the second search option (Option 2), i.e., beginning of the sector. In both cases above, first few bytes in the sense, length of the file header signature.

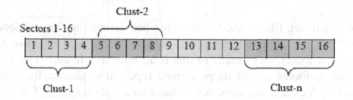

Fig. 2. Media representation with 4 sectors per cluster

It is also possible that a file can be embedded into another file i.e. picture files are embedded into document file and thumbs.db. In such a case both Options 1 and 2 cannot find the header signature, and Option 3 may be used. A search is performed to locate the file header signature throughout the sector.

To carve out files within a known file (for example document and thumbs.db file), a header signature search is performed only within that file which results in a faster carving process.

In case where digital media does not support a file system, Options 2 and 3 can be used.

3 Lost and Unallocated Clusters, Slack Space

A cluster is defined as a logical unit of file storage on a hard disk. Lost clusters are the clusters which are allocated to a file but are not having reference in the file allocation table. Lost clusters can result from files not being closed properly, from shutting down a computer without first closing an application (power failure) or from ejecting a storage medium, such as a floppy disk, from the disk drive while the drive is reading or writing.

Unallocated clusters are the clusters that are not allocated to any files on the hard disk according to the File Management System. These clusters can result from deleting a file or formatting the partition (or entire disk). While deleting a file or formatting the hard disk, data that is there in the clusters remains unchanged. If the resulted cluster in this case contains data, it is called a used unallocated cluster. If the data is not available, it is referred to as an unused unallocated cluster. A computer expert can identify and hide valuable information in these unallocated clusters.

Unused space in a disk cluster is defined as slack. The DOS and Windows file systems have fixed-size clusters. Even if the actual data being stored requires less storage than the cluster size, an entire cluster is reserved for the file. The unused space is called *slack space*. Slack space of the disk is mainly classified as file slack, partition slack, and disk slack. File slack and partition slack are always less than cluster size. Therefore, it is difficult for someone to hide an entire file in these slack spaces. Disk slack is slightly different from these two. There is no concept of cluster in disk slack. The space that is occupied by the set of sectors that are not coming as part of any partition of the disk is called disk slack. It can occur as a result of deleting a partition or leaving some part of a disk without partition.

4   Header/Footer Carving

This method of carving files is used when a file has defined header and footer. Jpeg, gif, png, html, pdf etc., may fall under this category. A file type can have more than one header and or footer, an example of that is an html file. In such a case searching for header and or footer should be performed repeatedly. Unique file headers and footers of various files that are supported by our tool are shown in the following table.

Table 1. Header, footer signatures

File	Header signature	Footer signature/ Method of carving
jpeg	FFD8	FFD9
gif	47494638	003B
png	89504E470D0A1A0A	49454E44
html	3C48544D4C3E	3C2F68746D6C3E
pdf	25504446	2525454F46
doc	D0CF11E0A1B11AE1	File structure based carving
ppt	”	”
excel	”	”
thumbs.db	”	”
zip	504B0304	”
bmp	424D	File size is embedded in the header
avi	52494646	”
dat	”	”
mp4	66747970	File structure based carving
mov	”	”
3gp	”	”
wmv	3026B2758E66CF11	”

Table 2. Jpeg segments

Hex	Symbol	Marker Name	Description
FFD8	SOI	Start of image	Start of compressed data
FFE1	APP1	Application Segment 1	Exif attribute information
FFE2	APP2	Application Segment 2	Exif extended data
FFDB	DQT	Define Quantization table	Quantization table definition
FFC4	DHT	Define Huffman table	Huffman table definition
FFDD	DRI	Define Restart Interoperability	Restart interoperability definition
FFC0	SOF	Start of Frame	Parameters relating to frame
FFDA	SOS	Start of Scan	Parameters relating to components
FFD9	EOI	End of Image	End of the compressed data

4.1 Carving JPEG Files

JPEG stands for Joint Photographic Experts Group, which is a standardization committee. It also stands for the compression algorithm that was invented by this committee. JPEG compressed images are often stored in a file format called JFIF (JPEG File Interchange Format). JPEG data structures are composed of segments (as shown in Table 2, that are marked by identifiers [4]. According to new JPEG [5] specifications, the new formats allow for multiple headers, footers and even nested images, to support thumbnails. Digital cameras often utilize the Application (APP) segment marker "0xffe1" to signify that they include more meta-data than the standard JFIF. The JPEG extraction algorithm need not search for footer from start of the header. Instead, it has to jump from the marker to marker until Start of Scan (SOS) marker.

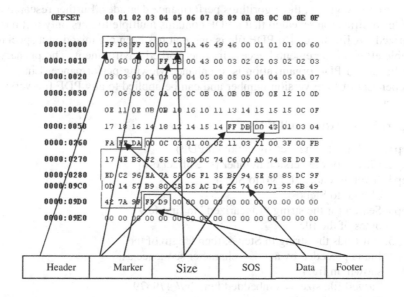

Fig. 3. Jpeg file format

The distance between any two consecutive markers is stored immediately after the first marker and that is two bytes in length. If the file is a valid JPEG then the last marker parsed will be the SOS marker, which signifies the beginning of the actual image data. Once this marker is reached then, our algorithm looks for the "0xffd9" marker, i.e., end of the image. This method of extraction increases the accuracy of extraction as well as the speed as entire headers are skipped instead of being processed by the searching algorithm. Figure 3 shows the data representation of jpeg file format with important markers.

5   Header/Embedded Length Carving

This method of carving files is used when a file has a distinct header and its length (file size) is stored in its first few bytes. Files that fall in this category are bmp, pdf, dat, avi, etc. This is one of the fastest carving methods used by our carving tool.

5.1   Carving PDF Files

PDF is a file format used to represent a document in a manner independent of the application software, hardware, and operating system used to create it [6]. A PDF file contains a PDF document and other supporting data. It is basically a binary file that also uses ASCII tags as delimiters to describe the header and trailer data structures in a Standard Generalized Markup Language (SGML) inspired fashion. A PDF file can have more than one footer signature. So, determining which footer actually represents the end of the file is a problem. As a result Kornblum and Kendall developed a REVERSE search mechanism [7] to find the last footer. The REVERSE method essentially looked for the last footer in the buffer and associated it with the given header.

As buffer size grows, the algorithms performance degrades. Further research of the PDF file specification revealed that a PDF contains multiple footers only if it has been "linearized". A linearized [6] PDF file is one that has been organized in a special way to enable efficient incremental access in a networked environment. The primary goal of the linearized PDF organization is to enhance viewing performance. Linearization is independent of PDF version number and can be applied to any PDF file version 1.1 or greater.

Algorithm to extract pdf Files

Step1. Look for the header signature (%PDF)
Step2. Check for the version number [file offset 6-8]
Step3. If version no. > 1.1 go to Step4
    Else go to Step6
Step4. Search for the string "Linearized" in first few
    bytes of the file
Step5. If it finds the string in Step 4, then length of the
    file is preceded by a "/L " character sequence as
    shown in fig.4
    Carved file size = embedded length;// 479579
    Else go to step6.

Step6. Use search algorithms to find footer signature
(%%EOF). Searching will be continued till
Carved file size<=User specified file size.

Note: - User specified file size is set by the user of the application to limit number of bytes to be carved. This is useful when a file does not have a defined footer signature.

The proposed algorithm is fast due to the fact that file size is often found within the first 100 bytes and no more file processing is necessary to extract linearized pdf files. In case a file is not linearized, a straightforward Boyer Moore search is performed to know the end of the file. Figure 4 shows the linearized pdf file header format.

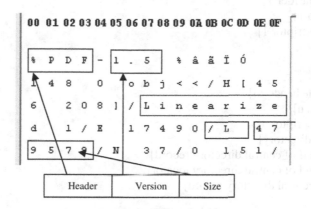

Fig. 4. Linearized pdf file header

6 File Structure Based Carving

This method of carving files is used when the internal structure of file is known. Files, which use this method of carving, are zip, compound document files (MS Document files, MS Power Point files, MS Excel files, etc) and video files (mp4, mov, 3gp, wmv). Compound document files are also called OLE (object linking and embedding) files. Compound document files work similar to real file systems. They contain a number of independent data *streams* (like files in a file system) that are organized in a hierarchy of *storages* (like sub directories in a file system) [12]. An example of file structure based carving along with the algorithm is explained the following section.

6.1 Carving Zip Files

Zip files often contain multiple embedded files of varying formats. ZIP archives are a standard format for compressing and storing multiple files [16]. Files are structured in an incremental fashion, followed by a "central directory structure" as shown in Figure 5 [9]. Each file contained within the zip has its own valid ZIP header with its compressed and uncompressed data sizes stored within it (Figure 6). This information can be exploited to increase the speed of the extraction of ZIP files.

The Zip file carving algorithm works incrementally by parsing each local file header (Figure 6). The next local file header offset is the summation of the compressed file size, file name length, extra length and the size of the data structure itself (30 bytes). The iteration will be continued until the beginning of the central directory (Figure 7). Then the Boyer Moore search is performed to locate the end of the central directory record (Figure 8). To find the end of zip file, the algorithm reads the length of the comment field at location 20 from the end of central directory.

```
[Local file header 1]
    [File data 1]
    [Data descriptor 1]
    .
    .
    .
    [Local file header n]
    [File data n]
    [Data descriptor n]
    [Central directory]
    [Zip64 end of central directory record]
    [Zip64 end of central directory locator]
    [End of central directory record]
```

Fig. 5. ZIP file format [9]

Local file header signature	**4ytes (0x504B0304)**
Version needed to extract	2 bytes
General purpose bit flag	2 bytes
Compression method	2 bytes
Last mod file time	2 bytes
Last mod file date	2 bytes
CRC-32	4 bytes
Compressed size	**4 bytes** [offset: 18]
Uncompressed size	4 bytes
File name length	2 bytes [offset: 26]
Extra field length	**2 bytes** [offset: 28]
File name	variable size
Extra field	variable size

Fig. 6. Local file header [9]

Central file header signature   4 bytes (0x504b0102)

Version made by	2 bytes
Version needed to extract	2 bytes
General purpose bit flag	2 bytes
Compression method	2 bytes
Last mod file time	2 bytes
Last mod file date	2 bytes
CRC-32	4 bytes
Compressed size	4 bytes
Uncompressed size	4 bytes
File name length	2 bytes
Extra field length	2 bytes
File comment length	2 bytes
Disk number start	2 bytes
Internal file attributes	2 bytes
External file attributes	4 bytes
Relative offset of local header	4 bytes
File name	(variable size)
Extra field	(variable size)
File comment	(variable size)

Fig. 7. Central directory record structure [9]

End of central dir signature   4 bytes (0x504b0506)

Number of this disk	2 bytes
Number of the disk with the start of the central directory	2 bytes
Total number of entries in the central directory on this disk	2 bytes
Total number of entries in the central directory	2 bytes
Size of the central directory	4 bytcs
Offset of start of central directory with respect to the starting disk number	4 bytes
Zip file comment length	**2 bytes** [offset: 20]
ZIP file comment	(variable size)

Fig. 8. End of central directory record structure [9]

Algorithm to extract zip files

Step1. Look for the header signature (**0x504B0304**)
Step2. Calculate the offset of next file header.
     (Next file header offset=compressed file size+file
   name length+extra length+30)

Step3. If content at the offset found in step2 is not
equal to beginning of the central directory
(**0x504b0102**) Go to Step2.
Else
Go to Step4.
Step4. Use search algorithms to find end of the
directory record (**0x504b0506**)
Step5. Get Zip file comment length at offset 20 from
the end of "end of the directory".
Step6. Offset of "end of the directory" and Zip file
comment length gives end of the Zip file.

7 Carving with Validation

This method of carving files is used when a file needs to be validated using a file type
specific validator. Files that use this validation method are gif, bmp, pdf, etc. This
method is used in combination with one of the other methods.

7.1 Carving GIF Files

GIF was the first image format introduced for the needs of the World Wide Web back
in 1987. Standing for Graphics Interchange Format, it represents a bitmap (graphics)
file format, which is based on the 2D raster data type and which supports a wide range
of resolutions [11]. There are two common versions of this format, 87a and 89a revi-
sion [10]. This format has remained unchanged for the last decade and thus has
proven to be a rather easy file to extract. It is one of the few that has a defined header
and footer. To carve a GIF file, one needs to acqure the file offsets of header and
footer. Before carving data between these two points, a test is performed to determine
if it is in fact a valid GIF file by looking for the versions "7a" or "9a". This kind of
validation minimizes false positives while carving.

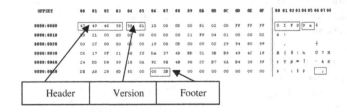

Fig. 9. GIF file format

8 Header/Maximum File Size Carving

This method of carving files is used when a file has a distinct header and does not a
have footer signature (or file that has footer, gets corrupted or overwritten). This is
also useful in carving files where the embedded length of the file gets overwritten.

In such a case, the carving file size is limited by the user specified file size. This method is very useful to get part of the file when the file footer gets corrupted, file is fragmented, or embedded file length is overwritten.

Note

1. For the file that does not have a standard footer and does not store file size in the header, the carved file size will be equal to the user specified file size.
2. For the file that has a standard footer and does not store the file size in the header, the carved file size will be:
   a. Less than the user specified file size, if the file footer is found before the user specified file size limit is reached during the search process.
   b. Equal to the user specified file size, otherwise.

9 Results

The proposed approach of data carving was applied on a number of digital images of varying sizes. Because of file fragments and part of file corruption due to over writing, the percentage of false positives observed was approximately 13%. The following table shows the statistics of carved files using this approach.

Table 3. Results

Digital Image Size	100% carved files	Partially carved files	% of correctly carved files
2GB	579	63	89.2
4GB	1745	198	88.7
8GB	4740	571	87.9
10GB	5090	721	85.9
20GB	13020	1511	88.4
Average % of correctly carved files = 87			

10 Conclusion

All carving methods defined in this paper work fine for files that have defined header and footer (or embedded file length) signatures. Unfortunately, not all file types have a standard footer signature, so determining the end of the file can be difficult. Carving sometimes may be time consuming, because only one carving method may not be sufficient for carving files like GIF, bmp, pdf etc. If a disk or digital media contains the file system, the proposed approach for data carving will be the best to carve files from lost clusters, unallocated clusters, slack space and a known file. This paper emphasizes on minimizing the time and search of carving files from digital media that does or does not support a file system.

Acknowledgement

The presented work is a part of National Cyber Forensics Resource Center initiative, funded by Department of Information Technology (DIT), Ministry of Communications and Information Technology (MCIT), Govt. of India. The goal of this initiative is to establish C-DAC, Trivandrum as one of the center of excellence for research and development in Cyber Forensics technology. We would like to thank Shri. Ramani. B, Adl. Derector, Shri. Thomas K.L, Jt. Director, Shri. Balan C, Dy. Director, C-DAC, Trivandrum, India, for providing constructive comments and help in improving the contents of this paper.

References

1. Statistical Disk Cluster Classification for File Carving, Cor J. Veenman. Intelligent System Lab, Computer Science Institute, University of Amsterdam, Amsterdam
2. Richard, G.G., Roussev, V.: Next-generation digital forensics. Communications of the ACM 49(2), 76–80 (2006)
3. Boyer, R.S., Moore, J.S.: A Fast String Searching Algorithm. Communications of the Association for Computing Machinery 20(10), 762–772 (1977)
4. Hamilton, E.: JPEG File Interchange Format, Version1.02.1 (September 1992)
5. Joint Photographic Experts Group, JPEG 2000 Specification (2004), http://www.jpeg.org/jpeg2000/ (last visited February 2009)
6. Adobe Systems Incorporated, Portable Document Format Reference Manual Version 1.3, March 11 (1999)
7. Naval Postgraduate School Thesis, Monterey, California, Nicholas Mikus (March 2005)
8. Digital Imaging Group, DIG2000 file format proposal, Appendix A (October 1998)
9. PKWARE Inc.: .ZIP File Format Specification Version: 6.2.0 (June 2004)
10. CompuServe Incorporated, Graphics Interchange Format (sm) (July 1990)
11. http://www.ntchosting.com/multimedia/ gif-graphics-interchange-format.html (June 2009)
12. Sun Microsystems. OpenOffice, http://www.openoffice.org/ (last visited: December 2009)
13. Wouters, W.: BMP Format (February 1997)
14. http://www.forensicswiki.org (last visited: March 2010)
15. http://www.webopedia.com (last visited: March 2010)
16. http://www.pkware.com/documents/casestudies/ (last visited: January 2010)

Semantic Modelling of Digital Forensic Evidence

Damir Kahvedžić* and Tahar Kechadi

Center for Cybercrime Investigations, University College Dublin, Dublin, Ireland
{damir.kahvedzic,tahar.kechadi}@ucd.ie

Abstract. The reporting of digital investigation results are traditionally carried out in prose and in a large investigation may require successive communication of findings between different parties. Popular forensic suites aid in the reporting process by storing provenance and positional data but do not automatically encode why the evidence is considered important. In this paper we introduce an evidence management methodology to encode the semantic information of evidence. A structured vocabulary of terms, ontology, is used to model the results in a logical and predefined manner. The descriptions are application independent and automatically organised. The encoded descriptions aim to help the investigation in the task of report writing and evidence communication and can be used in addition to existing evidence management techniques.

Keywords: Ontology Investigation Results Modelling Reporting.

1 Introduction

The Digital Investigation is becoming ever more complex with even small scale cybercrime investigations involving the analysis of multiple computers, flash disks, internet social networks, online accounts and mobile phones. Typically many tools may be used with results passed from one person to another during an investigation. The findings are typically reported in a prose document, detailing the steps taken, tools used and the interpretation of the results. As the size of the case grows, so does the complexity of its investigation and the description of the evidence. Once the case is concluded, the information is pooled together and presented to the relevant parties. Communication of the findings at each step in the process, in a clear, logical and reproducible manner is crucial for no evidence to be lost or miscommunicated. Current tools provide little context to the results they extract. The explanation of what the results imply, their relevance to the overall case, and where and how they relate to case events is all carried out in prose and may be prone to error.

In this paper we present a methodology to annotate results of digital investigative tools using a hierarchical vocabulary of computer forensics. The vocabulary provides context to the findings and allows the semantics and meaning of the results to be explicitly encoded. We use terms from DIALOG [9], a digital forensic ontology, developed to encompass knowledge associated with digital

---

* Financed by Irish Research Council for Science, Engineering and Technology, 2006.

I. Baggili (Ed.): ICDF2C 2010, LNICST 53, pp. 149–156, 2011.

forensics investigations. Describing evidence with the ontology involves instantiating relevant concepts and creating relationships between the individuals. The descriptions are textual, application independent and are used to supplement prose documents and existing evidence management techniques. The descriptions are easily merged and aggregated to form a complete view of the results. Further more, ontology specific processes, such as classifiers and inference engines, are employed to categorise the individuals and extract new knowledge. The ongoing development aims to supplement reporting procedures and relieve the investigator from manual descriptions of results with prose.

2   Previous Work

Managing, communicating and reporting of evidence is a crucial part of any investigation. Large forensic suites such as EnCase [4] highlight potential evidence and inserts them into report templates for quick dissemination of information. EnCase, for example, creates a web style report where the user browses through the findings in a similar manner to a web site. Bookmarks and hyperlinks are used to highlight significant information and lead the reader directly to where the evidence was found. A small number of bookmark types are available and allow both entire volumes as well as contents of files to be highlighted [1]. During the course of the investigation, users create hierarchical bookmark categories and place relevant evidence within them. The organisation is arbitrary and may result in logical inconsistencies where evidence should be in more than one category or are more applicable to one category rather than the other.

Bookmark information includes verbose structural, provenance and positional information only. Context, why the evidence is important and its meaning, is only specified in prose in the comment of the bookmark. Exchange of information between related parties and forensic suites is therefore limited to prose descriptions of evidence. Forensic tools cannot interpret prose without human intervention and therefore cannot automatically process the results further.

Forensic file formats have been developed to create such an exchangeable form of information across forensic applications. They provide compression, authentication and provenance to the data that was imaged. The formats often bundle images with a separate metadata component describing relevant case information [5,3,14,12]. The Sealed Digital Evidence Bag [12], used a set of limited ontologies to annotate the contents of individual evidence bags. The system first images the data and secondly records the details of the process and the evidence source by asserting properties from a predefined ontology.

Ontologies have been used to model arbitrary data in a number of domains [10]. In this work we are concerned with applying the logical structure of ontology [6] to evidence found during the course of the investigations. We use a hierarchical vocabulary of terms to allow the user to add semantic descriptions to arbitrary evidence. The ontology models all the results, including contents of files and events and automatically categorises them to relevant types. The evidence is categorised similarly to the EnCase bookmark categories but employs logical tools, such classifiers to verify the descriptions. The descriptions are stored in a separate file from the evidence image and provide an application independent and structured description of the case. Ontology descriptions are easily merged between tools and together create a rich description of the case.

In the rest of the paper we show how we utilise a digital forensics ontology, DIALOG [9], to describe the specific contents of the data. We use individuals and properties to annotate data and axioms and inference engines to classify them to relevant concepts. The hierarchical, logical and descriptive properties of ontology are utilised to organise the information in an application independent manner. The knowledge base can be explored and queried separately and supplements the creation of the final report.

3   Digital Investigation Concept

We use, DIALOG [9], a digital forensic ontology to describe forensic investigation results. It is a hierarchical metadata model describing concepts and the properties between them. The ontology can be regarded as a taxonomy of information with progressive restrictions (axioms) defining concepts down the hierarchy. DIALOG is defined using the ontology web language (OWL) and defines a single top level concept, the "*DigitalInvestigationConcept*". All other concepts are sub-classed from this parent, relate to associated concepts using defined properties and explicitly encoded a model of the forensics field. DIALOG has five main branches, the "*CrimeCase*", "*Information*" type, the "*Location*", the "*ForensicResource*" and the "*InvestigationActor*", each containing a hierarchy of concepts. The hierarchy is similar to the bookmark categories in EnCase but is predefined and more expressive since categories maintain links to related categories through predefined properties. Ontology can also leverage tools to process the information held within it.

Pellet [2], for instance, is an ontology reasoner that reclassifies individuals to the concepts whose axioms they satisfy. Based on the individual's properties, Pellet employs logical rules to find the concepts that the individual belongs to and may move the individual to more than one concept category. Therefore, to create any instance in the ontology, the user needs only to create an instance of a *DigitalInvestigationConcept* and annotate it with relevant properties. The Pellet inference engine would reclassify these individuals to the relevant concept. Alternatively, a sub-concept can be chosen, such as a *File*, and Pellet can specialise the individual to the specific *File* type *and* the generalise to the type of *Evidence* it is.

The definitions of concepts and properties are continually being expanded to increase the expressivity of the ontology. Our approach differs from [12] since we use inference mechanisms to automatically group and reclassify individuals.

All annotations are stored in a separate ontology file in OWL (Web Ontology Language). OWL has evolved from and is compatible with XML. Each instance occupies its own `<concept></concept>` block and connects to other instances with properties, also defined separately in concept blocks. Therefore, the annotations are supplementary to other investigation processes and referenced as an aid in creating the report. The following section describes how the evidence findings are encoded and how context is provided to the results.

4   Encoding of Results

In this section we illustrate how results from forensic tools are encoded in an ontology. The results instantiate relevant concepts, asserts properties and gives them a richer context than simple textual reporting. Each instance is named with a URI (Unique Resource Identifier) in the following format:

```
Format:  <namespace>:<asserted_type>-<Unique_Universal_ID>
Example: di:File-5038b43-511d-4381-9afe-c15d556b52c4
```

The <namespace>, locates the owl file that defines this individual. The default location is damir.ucd.ie\\DigitalInvestigation.owl. It is a blank ontology which simply imports all needed concepts and properties required for annotation. A copy is used locally for each result set and is modified to reflect the new location by editing the xml:base of the copy. The default namespace prefix is "di", but can also be modified in a similar manner. The "<asserted_type>" is a place holder for the individuals type. Additional types may be inferred by Pellet if the individual fulfil some concept properties. The "UUID" is a unique number. The instance name is verbose but designed to be unique. Typically, users would not see the underlying ID of an instance but some other more readable identifying information. For the rest of the paper, we use a shorthand notation, "di:File-5038b43", to refer to instances.

In the following we illustrate how we provide semantics to metadata, annotate file content and encode forensically relevant events. We model evidence found with tools built by our team [7,8] but results from other forensic tool can also be encoded. We describe a simple file, a document showing two people at some relevant location, that was found to be of evidentiary value.

4.1   Encoding Metadata

Metadata is loosely defined as data about data and used extensively by operating systems to provide rudimentary descriptions of specific information, such as files and folders. The metadata are simple tags and lack any structure, semantics or relationships. We encode these relationships using the concepts and properties from DIALOG and create a more richer description of the information.

For example, it is common to find files with names that relate to other concepts in the investigation. An image file, for instance, may be named after the person's portrait, the location that it was taken in, the event that it captures etc. Figure 1 shows how a simple scenario is encoded, where a filename is also a name of a person. Similar scenarios can occur if a filename is a name of an event or if the metadata reveals some other information.

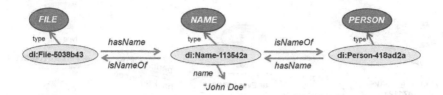

Fig. 1. Encoding Metadata Example

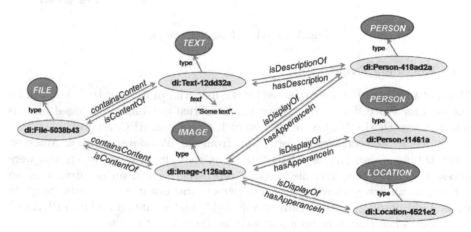

Fig. 2. Encoding Content Example

4.2   Encoding Content

Encoding the content of information concerns annotating the data container with the appropriate concepts that it holds information on. Data containers are defined as any object that contain other data. Here, we take the *File* as an illustrating example but we use the same method to describe other containers, such as the *Folder* or *RegistryValue*. Semantically, files cannot contain physical objects, rather they contain *evidence of* physical objects stored in some format. There is no restriction on the number of different information a file can hold. An email file, may contain a number of emails stored in a cascading format and a word processing file may contain both text, images and emails. Therefore, to describe the content of a file in DIALOG, the user first specifies the contents of the file, an image for example, then describes what the content is evidence of.

Figure 2 shows an encoding of the content of our example file. It contains an image and some text. The image display two people at a location, the person the file was named after and the person that created it. The various concepts are further annotated to describe them in more detail but are not present in the figure. These include the address of the location for example, the specific text that was found to be relevant and the location (page number) of the elements within the file.

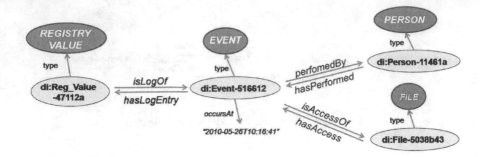

Fig. 3. Encoding Events Example

4.3   Encoding Events

Metadata and content are extracted by the majority of forensic tools and can be encoded as above. Event reconstruction is carried out implicitly based on this information. DIALOG also encodes event information. RPCompare [9] is a tool developed to extract event information from the Windows registry. Amongst other things, it can analyse MRU lists to extract the order of which files were accessed across time. The file accesses represent Events, an occurrence of an action, which are performed by some person and occur at a specific point in time. Time ontologies are already specified [15] and are integrated into DIALOG to encode when the event occurs as well as the order of events.

Figure 3 shows an example of how a *FileAccess* event is encoded. The *is-LoggedBy* property links the source of the evidence to the actual event. In this case it is an MRU registry value. The figure omits any relationships, such as *hasName* and *isInRegistryKey* that the instance also asserts. Access events of external devices, operating systems or other data is similarly encoded. The event ontology also supports the description of deletion events, creation events and can be expanded incrementally for other event types. The creation of the example file by the user (*"di:Person-11461a"*) is encoded in that manner.

5   Data Retrieval and Implementation

Once data is annotated within the ontology it can be readily manipulated and explored with ontology specific operations. Pellet, for example, manages the information and infers the category of every instance by testing them against concept axioms. For example, although file *"di:File-5038b43"* was asserted to be only an instance of a file, due to its properties it was inferred that it is also an instance of a *ImageFile, UserFile, MultimediaFile, MultimediaEvidence* amongst other concepts. Similarly, the various events are inferred to be *FileAccessedEvent, FileCreationEvent* etc. Additionally, the hierarchy of DIALOG groups instances to parent concepts and allows the individuals to be accessed through parent nodes. The grouping of similar evidence types simplifies the exploration of the knowledge. The knowledge can subsequently be explored either manually or by querying the information.

The ontology query language, SQWRL, is used to query for specific evidence. The query below, for example, queries for any elements that contain evidence of both the people used in the previous examples. It retrieves evidence that was found to prove that person A had some connection with person B. The query uses the DIALOG property *isComponentOf* which is a transitive super property of *isLogOf*, *isNameOf*, *isDisplayOf* used in the examples above. The query applies to all of them and only returns instances that satisfy the conditions. In the example above, the query returns the instance of image, "*di:Image-1126aba*", that was found to contain pictures of both the persons, it can be similarly used to extract conversations, events etc. that both agents took part in.

```
inf:isComponentOf(?di:x, di:Person-11461a)    ^
inf:isComponentOf(?di:x, di:Person-418ad2a)  ->
sqwrl:select(?di:x)
```

As well as querying the knowledge, the information can be explored manually. Since ontology descriptions are written in an extension of XML, existing XML editors can be used to explore the underlying data. Some ontology specific editors exist to interpret and present OWL information [13].

We have implemented a new ontology editing environment that is used to describe results found by forensic tool in the manner illustrated above. The environment can aggregate results from multiple sources to a central location and allow the exploration of the data in a variety of ways. It allows the user to query the information as above or explore it manually through either a grid or "linked-graph" manner. A number of operations have been implemented to allow the user to concentrate on specific evidence or properties of evidence. The graph view in particular allows the information to be viewed in a similar way to how ontology is visualised in the figures of this paper.

Our ongoing work will concentrate on simplifying the user interface to reduce the amount of effort required for data input and an exporting feature to report findings. Reporting entails parsing the instances and following their properties. The extracted text will be similar to prose and can be used to supplement existing reporting procedures.

6   Conclusion

In this paper we illustrated the ongoing development of an evidence management and reporting methodology for digital forensics. We use a digital investigation ontology to model metadata, file content and event evidence in an application independent and semantic manner. The descriptions provide context to the data and allows the evidence to be explored in an intuitive way. The methodology is similar to the bookmarking system of many forensic suites, in that evidence is progressively tagged during the course of the investigation, but differs in the fact that it is structured, application independent and annotates the meaning of evidence rather than its structure and position.

Ontology mechanisms, such as inference, classification and catagorisation, are used to manage the data and group instances together for easy understanding, exploring and querying. Future directions of the research include development of a reporting tool that parses asserted information and creates prose like text. Addition of general vocabularies such as WordNet [11] will also be carried out to add more expressivity to the descriptions.

References

1. Bunting, S.: EnCase Computer Forensics: EnCe The Official EnCase Certified Examiner Study Guide, 2nd edn., Sybex (2008)
2. Pellet, http://clarkparsia.com/pellet/ (visited: May 2010)
3. Cohen, M., Garfinkel, S., Schatz, B.: Extending the advanced forensic format to accommodate multiple data sources, logical evidence, arbitrary information and forensic workflow. Digital Investigation 6, 57–68 (2009)
4. Encase, http://www.guidancesoftware.com/ (visited: May 2010)
5. Garfinkel, S.L., Malan, D.J., Dubec, K.A., Stevens, C.C., Pham, C.: Disk imaging with the advanced forensic format, library and tools. In: Research Advances in Digital Forensics (2nd Ann. IFIP WG 11.9 Int. Conf. on Digital Forensics). Springer, Heidelberg (2006)
6. Gruber, T.R.: Toward principles for the design of ontologies used for knowledge sharing. Int. Jrnl. of Human-Computer Studies 43, 907–928 (1995)
7. Kahvedžić, D., Kechadi, T.: Extraction and Categorisation of User Activity from Windows Restore Points. Jrnl. of Digital Forensics, Security and Law 4 (2008)
8. Kahvedžić, D., Kechadi, T.: Correlating Orphaned Windows Registry Data Structures. In: ADFSL 2009, Proc. of the Conf. on Digital Forensics, Security and Law, pp. 67–81 (2009)
9. Kahvedžić, D., Kechadi, T.: DIALOG: A Framework for Modelling, Analysis and Reuse of Digital Forensic Knowledge. Digital Investigation 6, 23–33 (2009)
10. Semantic Web Case Studies and Use Cases, http://www.w3.org/2001/sw/sweo/public/UseCases/ (visited: May 2010)
11. Miller, G.A.: WordNet: A Lexical Database for English. Comm. of the ACM 38, 39–41 (1995)
12. Schatz, B., Clark, A.: An open architecture for digital evidence integration. In: Proc. of the 2006 AusCERT Asia Pacific Information Technology Security Conference R&D Stream, pp. 15–29 (2006)
13. Protégé Ontology Editor and Knowledge Acquisition System, http://protege.stanford.edu/ (visited: May 2010)
14. Turner, P.: Applying a forensic approach to incident response, network investigation and system administration using digital evidence bags. Digital Investigation 4, 30–35 (2007)
15. Time Ontology in OWL, http://www.w3.org/TR/2006/WD-owl-time-20060927/ (visited: May 2010)

Author Index

Printed in the United States
By Bookmasters